businessbuddies

**success in
dealing with**

difficult
people

For further success in all aspects of
business, be sure to read these
other businessbuddies books:

Successful Assertive Management
Successful Negotiating
Successful Leadership Skills
Successful Interviews
Successful Performance Reviews

businessbuddies

success in dealing with
difficult people

difficult
people

Ken Lawson, M.A., Ed.M.

BARRON'S

First edition for the United States, its territories and dependencies, and Canada published 2006 by Barron's Educational Series, Inc.

Conceived and created by
Axis Publishing Limited
8c Accommodation Road
London NW11 8ED
www.axispublishing.co.uk

Creative Director: Siân Keogh
Editorial Director: Anne Yelland
Design: Sean Keogh, Simon de Lotz
Managing Editor: Conor Kilgallon
Production: Jo Ryan, Cécile Lerbière

NOTE: The opinions and advice expressed in this book are intended as a guide only. The publisher and author accept no responsibility for any loss sustained as a result of using this book.

All inquiries should be addressed to:
Barron's Educational Series, Inc.
250 Wireless Boulevard
Hauppauge, New York 11788
www.barronseduc.com

Library of Congress Control No: 2004116961

ISBN-13: 978-0-7641-3248-3
ISBN-10: 0-7641-3248-2

Printed and bound in China
9 8 7 6 5 4 3 2 1

contents

6

Introduction

We all have a story to tell about a colleague or a boss who makes the workplace a bit more challenging than you'd like it to be. Although there are as many types of difficult behavior as there are people, you will probably recognize some of the following: The hostile and aggressive types, who are abusive, intimidating, and arrogant; the complaining types, who find fault with everything, and never hesitate to say so; the unresponsive or silent types, who are bland and non-committal; the superagreeable types, who are ever eager to please but can never keep a promise; the negative types, who throw a damper on all new ideas; and the know-it-all expert types, who need to be totally right, 24/7.

You interact with them every day. You work on projects with them and attend meetings with them. Perhaps you talk about them with other colleagues. Perhaps you complain to your friends and family about them when the workday's done. Perhaps you argue with them in your mind's eye. Or, shocking though it might seem, perhaps you are one of them.

Success in Dealing with Difficult People profiles these challenging workplace personalities, explains what makes them tick, and outlines what you can do to cope with them. Through the clear, concise ideas on these pages, you'll understand what behaviors these personalities bring into the workplace, and how to guard against them. You'll learn how to respond constructively to difficult co-workers and you'll see a host of guidelines for working successfully alongside them in your everyday work environment.

First, you'll learn how to identify and understand difficult behaviors, and the significance of different workplace priorities and contexts. You'll also see how and where your own actions fit into the picture. After, you'll read about the personality profiles of difficult colleagues, and the toxic behaviors they infuse into the workplace.

Then come dozens of tips for confronting difficult behaviors, along with a host of coping strategies that you can put to use immediately in your workplace. You'll learn, for example, how to counter difficult behavior in

8

Introduction continued

meetings and other situations, using effective listening and speaking skills that are clearly explained, easy to master, and that have been proven to work.

Workers fall into two categories: Bosses and employees. First, you'll learn about the profiles of difficult bosses, and see strategies for dealing with them effectively. You'll no doubt have seen these bosses in action, perhaps more often than you'd care to recall: The aggressive boss; the hands-on boss; the hands-off boss; the weak boss; and the political boss. See what drives their personalities and how to interact successfully with them.

On the flip side of the coin are difficult employees. If you're a manager of people, you'll recognize unproductive employee behaviors such as time-wasting, slowness, finger-pointing, and dishonesty, among many others. Here, you'll learn the smart strategies that will equip you to deal with these behaviors (and others), along with tips and advice for managing key interpersonal situations effectively, to produce the best possible outcome.

Finally, you'll learn how to deal productively with difficult customers.

You'll gain a host of valuable tips on confronting customer crises, dealing with dissatisfactions, and keeping loyalty and goodwill at the foundation of your business relations.

Wherever individuals congregate, potential for conflict lurks. Difficult personalities are everywhere, yet the workplace provides a particularly alluring stage for the drama they create. You may never be able to avoid difficult people and their challenging behaviors at work, but you can deal with them strategically and successfully if you know how—which is exactly what this book will teach you.

Ken Lawson, M.A., Ed.M.
Career management counselor and author
Instructor, School of Continuing and Professional Studies
New York University

1

understanding
difficult behavior

The benefits

There are many good reasons why you can benefit from dealing successfully with difficult people.

1 DIFFICULT STAFF CAN PROVE COSTLY
If as a manager you're unable to deal with problem behavior and end up firing an employee, you could be setting your company up for some hefty legal fees. Even if you dismiss someone for what you feel are legitimate reasons, the employee can file for wrongful dismissal. Even though most lawsuits are futile, they still take up company time and money.

2 PROBLEM EMPLOYEES CAN AFFECT THE BOTTOM LINE
Even if you don't resort to firing, difficult employees may well end up being the greatest unmeasured cost to your business. Although it's very difficult to quantify the cost of keeping problem people, you can guarantee they are hindering the smooth running of your business and, hence, overall profitability. They also bring down morale and productivity among dedicated employees.

3 IGNORING DIFFICULT BEHAVIOR WILL BACKFIRE IN THE LONG RUN
Disconnecting from the problem behavior may reduce your stress
for a short time but the negative consequences on other staff and
your own business objectives will end up being corrosive.

4 PUT YOURSELF IN THE DRIVER'S SEAT
Remember that you will always face individuals who adopt
difficult behavior and the sooner you are able to interpret the
signs and improve your communication skills, the fewer
opportunities problem people will have to coerce, manipulate,
or intimidate you in the future.

The benefits continued

5 TURN PROBLEM STAFF INTO A PROFITABLE ASSET
It's quite a challenge to transform people's most irritating habits (often linked closely with their greatest strengths) into a valuable, resourceful, and hopefully revenue-making asset.

6 FACING AND RESOLVING PROBLEM STAFF HELPS YOUR OVERALL CONFIDENCE
When you face and resolve the problem yourself, you feel like you are in control. By conquering the opposition, you also conquer your fear. Few accomplishments are more satisfying than confronting a difficult person with success.

7

A DIFFICULT BOSS CAN GET RID OF YOU
If as an employee you fail to settle a dispute with a difficult boss, you put yourself in a vulnerable position where you are cast in the role of a troublemaker or incompetent and risk being passed over for promotion or, at worst, losing your job.

8

YOU WILL LEARN NEW LIFE SKILLS
Shying away from difficult people will not help you develop personally. Difficult people exist in all walks of life, and we have to deal with them on a daily basis. Never fully addressing how to deal with them will hamper your growth as a strong, capable person.

Defining difficult behavior

What is the definition of a difficult person? The answer will be influenced by your own type of personality, your history with the so-called problem person, your experience with similar personalities, your position in the company compared with theirs, and the length of time you have known the person. In short, a multitude of subjective and highly personal factors come into play in defining what makes a difficult person. One person's impossible colleague could well prove another's dream co-worker.

REMEMBER:

1 FOCUS ON BEHAVIOR, NOT PEOPLE
If you are lucky, there may be a general consensus within a company as to who is a troublesome person. But more often than not, if you took a poll from the people around you and asked for their definition of a difficult person, you would get just as many versions as the number of people you surveyed.

That's why it's more useful to talk about difficult behavior than difficult people.

This prevents any criticism of behavior from being perceived as a personal or biased attack. Focusing on particular instances of difficult behavior also allows the people involved in the conflict, as well as any observers, to take a more objective look at the situation.

2

DIFFERENCES CREATE DIFFICULTIES
In fact, the very diversity of perspectives and working styles
that are inevitably present in a working team are most
frequently the source of conflict that participants describe as
"difficult behavior." In many cases, a manager's definition of a
difficult person is an individual whose work style is different
from his own. For instance, a person who is meticulous about
research and fact-checking may clash with an action-oriented
individual who puts a greater emphasis on getting a job
done quickly.

In this case, both individuals bring a different set of tools and
attitudes to a particular task. Although they follow correctly
their own working methods to achieve results, their different
perspectives may lead them to see the other as an obstacle—
in other words, a difficult person.

It requires a skillful manager to appreciate workers'
complementary skills and to minimize the ground for conflict
by allocating individual talents to suitable roles.

Defining difficult behavior continued

WHAT KIND OF PERSON ARE YOU?

1 Do you like to work closely with people and enjoy a team experience?

2 Or do you relish individual research arriving at conclusions on your own?

3 Or do you prefer to work off the cuff and thrive on being forced to make swift decisions?

Whatever your response, consider the circumstances under which your particular working style, and the way you project your character and personality to those around you could be perceived by team members as difficult behavior. Conversely, consider which of your colleagues' working methods most irritate you. Are you sure that you are justified in your reaction to a different way of working?

Identifying difficult behavior

The sooner you can identify which bosses, co-workers, and employees will display the most difficult behavior, the greater your chances will be of success in resolving conflicts that are likely to absorb your time and energy.

THERE ARE TWO MAIN WAYS OF IDENTIFYING DIFFICULT BEHAVIOR:

1 Observing and annotating people's behavior in the workplace

2 Linking your findings with the impact this behavior has on you

There are some standard telltale signs of a person under stress. Watch and take notice if you've spotted the following behavior on at least three occasions. Try and identify if this is a onetime or a pattern. Try also to understand that we all have off days, or go through short periods of intense stress at work. It is important to differentiate between a consistent behavioral trait, and one that is simply temporarily out of character.

STRESS SIGNALS:

1 Flashes of quick temper

2 A visible lack of attention to personal appearance

3 A lack of focus on a task/easily distracted

4 Frequent comments about fatigue

5 Excessive eating at work or failure to take lunch breaks

6 Failure to make a deadline

Identifying difficult behavior continued

In addition, many difficult people generate their negative behavior from personality traits that are not immediately visible. Often, people who appear to be model employees end up being devious, calculating, or controlling. The following situations suggest difficult people are having a negative impact at work:

1 Genuinely good ideas are failing to deliver the results that are expected.

2 Certain people have value and experience but also nagging or ongoing problems associated with them.

3 In the presence of certain people, you don't seem to think, communicate, or operate as clearly.

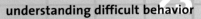
4 You have difficulty getting clear feedback from certain staff.

5 You experience difficulty getting real commitment from or handling certain people effectively.

6 Some people seem to know exactly how to ruffle your normally smooth feathers.

7 There are situations when you are made to feel out of control.

Identifying difficult behavior continued

8 A team member is stopping you from achieving an objective in time.

9 A colleague often ends up making you feel guilty.

10 After meeting a certain colleague, you are regularly left with negative thoughts.

11 Some people appear helpful but end up creating extra work for you and others.

12 A co-worker is consistently highly critical of others.

13 The boss is more self-protective than supportive.

14 A colleague likes to disrupt board meetings but fails to provide any positive input.

15 You start avoiding certain colleagues or your boss because you assume that they will create problems for you.

Understanding your own behavior

After you've identified the signs of problem behavior, you face the more probing task of understanding the reasons for the behavior. Fine tune your diagnosis by taking a look at your own behavior.

SIGNS YOU ARE UNDER STRESS:

1 You clench your jaw, you're short of breath, you feel sluggish, or you perspire more than normal.

2 You are prone to bouts of apathy, impatience, sudden outbursts of rage, or restlessness.

3 You work on weekends.

4 You don't take time to eat during the working day.

5 You don't take time off when you're ill.

6 You resent other people taking time off.

7 You don't take annual leave because you can't find anyone to stand in for you when you're away.

8 If you do go on vacation, you take work with you.

9 You find yourself collapsing with exhaustion during the weekend.

10 It's a long time since you made some time for old friends and family.

Your attitudes toward difficult people

You may discover that the issue, the conflict, the misunderstanding or whatever it is that's frustrating you about your problem employee is actually a reflection of something in you. Three possible scenarios are given here.

1 You see something in them that you dislike about yourself. For example, if you notice that an employee is weak under pressure, it's probably reminding you of some vulnerability inside you.

2 The person is drawing attention to a skill that you have yet to master. For instance, if the employee is painfully slow, you may need to learn patience.

3 The person is highlighting aspects of yourself (for instance pride or fear) that you don't want to confront. If the person is a rebel who is questioning your authority, you may have to stand back and drop your need to have absolute control of a situation.

PONDER THESE SCENARIOS WHEN YOU ANSWER THE FOLLOWING
QUESTIONS ABOUT YOUR ATTITUDES TOWARD PEOPLE YOU FIND DIFFICULT

1 Have you always experienced difficulty with the same type
of person or actions?

2 Does a pattern exist for you in your interaction with
co-workers? Do you recognize that you have hot buttons
that are easily pushed?

3 Is the difficult person always behaving badly or are they just
having a bad day?

4 Are you sure you're not reacting negatively to practically
everything they do because something about their appearance
(for instance, hair, moustache, perfume, mannerisms) remind
you of an unpleasant person in your past?

Are you encouraging difficult behavior?

Could your actions or attitudes contribute to other people's difficult behavior? Below are some recommendations to help you take charge of your reactions instead of letting your instincts control you.

1 The next time something or someone makes you feel negative, try not to get trapped into thinking you have to please the other person. Don't be defensive or lash back.

2 Try to evaluate whether the feeling (depression, anger, pain, guilt, frustration, jealousy, weakness) the difficult person provokes in you, is realistic. Will your response help you maintain control over the situation?

3 Explore what you are seeing in this person that mirrors something deep inside you that you don't want to face.

4 Distance yourself from the person by taking a detached, impersonal view. The more you can see her as separate from yourself, the less likely you'll be to interpret her behavior as a personal attack against you. You probably have nothing to do with her behavior.

5 Try to appreciate your differences and work out how your different skills and viewpoints can complement each other and enhance the work you do on a project.

Understanding other people's behavior

A greater understanding of what makes you tick should help you identify the possible causes for people's bad behavior. The following are descriptions of three basic types of behavior patterns that most workers adopt. Most people switch from one mode of operating to another depending on the situation.

1 PASSIVE BEHAVIOR

People who rarely express their real opinions, desires, and needs are passive. They usually give in to the wishes of others. They hardly ever stand up for themselves. Because they show a lack of respect for themselves, they become easy prey for more proactive types.

OUTCOME: Passive people can end up feeling angry and resentful that others are taking advantage of them. This can prey on already low levels of self-esteem and self-confidence. Introverted types find it difficult to let off steam at work so they are more likely to express the dissatisfaction by taking days off sick.

2 AGGRESSIVE BEHAVIOR
People who show little respect for other people's wishes or opinions are regarded as aggressive. They are determined to get their own way on big and small issues.

OUTCOME: Behind a pushy exterior, aggressive people can be insecure. They can also make others feel humiliated, defensive, or just downright tired.

3 ASSERTIVE BEHAVIOR
People who feel at ease expressing their needs and standing their ground are assertive. They like to take positive action and blend their direct, confident approach with respect for others.

OUTCOME: Working with assertive people instills confidence, spreads enthusiasm and energy, and encourages co-operation.

OVERVIEW
People exhibit varying degrees of all three patterns at different times. People are considered as problematic when they chose to adopt extremes of behavior. The extremes do not have to be just related to aggression— excesses of passivity can be just as problematic for managers.

Understanding different contexts

People's behavior patterns and priorities are not preprogrammed and can vary considerably depending on different contexts. Some of the most common destabilizing contexts are a change in management team, a company takeover, or a relocation.

CHANGING CONTEXTS

1 NEW PRIORITIES
Most people strive to do a good job, but sometimes the effort to provide a speedy service will mean sacrificing total accuracy, careful analysis, and elaborate planning. For perfectionists and sticklers to detail, getting the job right is the ultimate goal, and these people dislike being pressured by time demands.

2 CONFUSION
When a period of change is either poorly communicated to staff or badly anticipated, the outcome is confusion. In the absence of information, the rumor mill takes over, adding the fuel of speculation to the reigning confusion. Some people may think their share of responsibilities and workload goes up and feel incapable of handling the extra work. Others believe they are underutilized and lack motivation to push themselves at work.

TIPS TO AVOID THE NEGATIVE EFFECTS OF CHANGE AND CONFUSION

1 Never forget the emotional responses through which people go during a time of upheaval and possible job losses.

2 Inform people as much as possible as to the changes, dispel rumors, let them understand why things are changing and what it means for them.

3 Listen to their anxieties; be understanding and supportive.

4 Don't underestimate how even the most trivial changes in an office can affect morale.

Understanding different priorities

Workers have diverging goals and motivations. In a team context, this can also create conflict. A skillful manager will be aware of these differences and orchestrate them to benefit the company's main objectives.

MAIN PRIORITIES

1
GETTING A JOB DONE
Deadlines are necessary in most businesses but especially in the media, publishing, and retail world where swift access to information or goods is essential. Urgent action demands a direct, decisive hands-on approach.

2
GETTING ALONG WITH PEOPLE
Relating well to people is key to service and tourism industries. Companies whose goal is to provide either a swift or highly valued service may prove alienating for people whose main commitment is to provide friendly customer service or to operate within a friendly, open environment.

CHECKLIST FOR MANAGERS

1 DEALING WITH DIFFICULT PEOPLE TESTS YOUR MANAGEMENT SKILLS
Learning how to transform problem staff into valuable
workers is a key management skill.

2 DON'T MAKE IT PERSONAL
There are dangers with defining difficult people, so focus on
difficult behavior because it enables you to be objective.

3 UNDERSTAND YOUR OWN BIAS
It's easy to jump to conclusions about other people's ways of
working. Think about your own behavior and evaluate to what
extent it is influencing your opinion.

4 LOOK AT CAUSES OF DIFFICULT BEHAVIOR
The most instinctive responses to situations are aggression or
passivity. Remember that workers have different motivations
and their responses change according to different contexts.

KEY QUESTIONS

dealing with difficult
types & behaviors

Overview

Although there are general principles and rules that can be applied to confronting difficult behavior, it's necessary to fine tune your communications skills depending on the type of difficult person or behavior you are facing. Below is a list of difficult types and behaviors that you are likely to encounter on a daily basis. Most people adopt some of these characteristics in varying degrees at some stages of their working life. It's important for you to be highly alert to these features in yourself and other people and to make sure they don't become obstacles to your working goals.

DIFFICULT TYPES

1 Hostile/aggressive

2 Complainer

3 Unresponsive/silent

4 Super-agreeable

5 Negativist

6 Know-it-all expert

Overview continued

BEHAVIOR TO WATCH OUT FOR

1 Arrogance

2 Impatience

3 Obstinacy

4 Self-deprecation

5 Self-destruction

6 Martyrdom

7 Sniping

8 Anger

9 Indecision

PERSONALITY TYPES AND PROBLEM BEHAVIORS
The remainder of the chapter deals with the most common personality types and difficult behaviors you are likely to encounter. They will show you how to recognize them and how to cope with the impact they cause in the workplace.

Hostile/aggressive

HOW TO RECOGNIZE

- They are bullies who always need to be in the right.

- They are abusive, abrupt, intimidating, arbitrary, as well as arrogant.

- They appear self-confident and look down on those more uncertain than themselves.

- They fly off the handle in an instant.

- They are happiest when they are running the show.

- They make direct attacks.

HOW TO COPE

1

Don't run in the other direction. Show them you're not intimidated. They will respect you more if you are assertive. They may even be testing you. Aggressive people have low tolerance for passive behavior.

2 Avoid out-and-out war. These people tend to love a fight and the experience of winning. They will be less adept at confronting you if you remain calm yet assertive.

3 Stick to facts. A cool, polite "I disagree with you for these reasons" will take the wind out of their sails. Steer away from any opinions, however small. Give them no reason to pick up a new argument. That's their favorite hobby.

4 If they talk while you are speaking, keep repeating their names until they respond.

5 Once you've got their attention, make your point quickly and firmly. Repeat the same point if necessary to be sure they focus their thoughts.

Hostile/aggressive continued

6 Try playing back what they've been angry about. It shows you are taking them seriously.

7 Sometimes it's best to let them vent their anger and then have your say. They may surprise you and become reasonable once their tantrum is over.

8 Don't be afraid to admit to a mistake.

9 Maintain eye contact.

10 Get them to sit down and don't sit down yourself until they do.

11 If possible, allow them to save face. Bullies are highly sensitive (if only about themselves). Suggest a few alternative solutions. Let them know that you won't tolerate a repeat outburst.

Complainer

HOW TO RECOGNIZE

- They find fault with everything, creating an atmosphere of general negativity.

- They blame everyone else.

- They love making accusations about colleagues.

- They come across as perfect and love playing the victim.

HOW TO COPE

1 Don't insist on trying to solve their problems. They'll hate the idea that the self-fulfilling cycle of passivity and blaming may come to an end. They'll offer extra resistance.

2 Take their complaints seriously by asking them to put it in writing. Ask lots of open-ended questions. Make sure they quantify their complaints.

3 Pay attention to them. They may be complaining to get attention they don't think they are getting.

4 Listening doesn't mean agreeing. Remain neutral until you've gathered all the facts.

5 Ask them to be specific about their complaints. Often what they're choosing to complain about isn't the only source of their grievances.

6 Their nit-picking can be very useful when it draws attention to potential problems that others have passed over or don't want to point out.

7 Suggest things you know they can look forward to.

8 Don't stop asking questions.

Unresponsive/silent

HOW TO RECOGNIZE

■ They don't express any opinions, even when asked. Don't think this means they don't have an opinion.

■ When they are coaxed into an opinion, it will be noncommittal. This may make you suspect they, in fact, disagree with you even if they don't.

■ They will sit quietly in meetings, adding nothing. This can appear intimidating: Are they dismissing everyone's opinions? Are they bored? Are they keeping their wisdom to themselves?

■ Silence can be deliberately unhelpful. When this is the case, keeping quiet is aggressive.

HOW TO COPE

1 Pay attention to them. They may be complaining to get attention they don't think they are getting.

2 Steer away from questions that generate "yes" or "no" answers. Keep questions open-ended. "How" and "Why" will force them to give some explanation.

3 Make sure your body language is encouraging them to answer. Tilt your head forward; raise your eyebrows expectantly.

4 Don't fill awkward silences with your words. That lets them off the hook. Ask them instead whether they agree with what you've just said. Comment even on the fact that they are not communicating. "You seem annoyed, impatient?" forces them to express a feeling.

5 At a meeting, explain that you expect everyone to contribute. Ask people to talk in turn around the table for instance.

6 If silence persists, keep smiling, even if you're faced by glares, frowns, or shrugs. Tell them their opinions matter to you.

7 Once they start speaking, don't interrupt or move on swiftly to another point. You're trying to encourage future participation. Show them you are counting on them.

Super-agreeable

HOW TO RECOGNIZE

■ They are ready with a smile, attentive, and eager to please.

■ They make lots of promises and volunteer help. But don't count on them to fulfill their promises. They may have said the same thing to everyone in the department.

■ They don't seem to think of the consequences of their over-committing themselves to tasks and people.

■ They tell you what you want to hear. It's flattering the first few times, then you start questioning their sincerity.

■ They avoid all conflict, even if they are being bullied.

HOW TO COPE

1 Don't blame them directly for letting you down. The reason they are so agreeable is that they dread conflict so a ticking-off will only intensify their eagerness to please.

2 Encourage them to make opinions. Let them know whatever they think won't jeopardize their relationship with you. Let them know it is safe to be honest.

3 When you ask them for an opinion, ask them to back up their statements. Find out why they seem to approve or agree with you.

4 If they continue to commit themselves easily, ask them to put their commitment down in writing. Emphasize that it is important to you that they meet the deadline.

Super-agreeable continued

5 Ask other colleagues whether they've taken on work and make sure that they haven't taken on more than they can handle.

6 If they still can't say no, give them very structured, no-nonsense assignments.

7 When they do disappoint you by delivering work late, let them know. Appeal to their eagerness to please. It may mortify them enough to have let you down that they will be more thoughtful of committing themselves the next time.

8 When they have let you down, ask them what they might do differently next time. This encourages them to improve their behavior, rather than dwell on their present mistakes.

9 Show them you appreciate results. This will help them focus on achievements rather than on making promises.

10 Provide recognition for tasks that have been completed on time. This avoids a consistently negative message and encourages future success.

Negativist

HOW TO RECOGNIZE

- They tend to throw cold water on any idea.

- They appear angry and resentful most of the time.

- They'll always find a reason why something could go wrong.

- They are convinced they have little power over their own lives and those that do are not to be trusted.

- They don't believe that things can improve.

- They can be perfectionists, reminding you of small details you have overlooked in your general enthusiasm. They are usually idealists. They are more likely to point out why something was not as good as it could have been than why it's inherently bad.

HOW TO COPE

1 Be aware of how you can become vulnerable to negative remarks around you. Negative people love to spread their negativity around to prove to themselves that they are right. Remain optimistic.

2 Avoid arguing with them. They'll only rise to the occasion and paint an even worse picture.

3 Steer instead to the facts. Ask them to back their sweeping generalizations with examples. Challenge these examples in a calm manner.

4 Don't argue with them or embarrass them. You won't get far by making it a "win/lose" battle.

5 Turn them into a sounding board. They could bring a useful dose of realism to a project. Listen to their advice—if they are sticking to facts, that is. They could prove an invaluable resource.

6 Remind them of past successes. Ask for instance: "Do you remember when we achieved x?"

58

Know-it-all expert

HOW TO RECOGNIZE

- They are always right. This could be an asset for your company. What detracts from their know-it-all expertise is that they'll never fail to remind you of it.

- They may not mean to, but they can easily make you and others look foolish.

- They can be pompous and condescending.

- They are often knowledgeable and highly competent. They thrive on being challenged as it presents them with an opportunity to show off their expertise.

- When a job has to be done quickly, they can slow the process down by nit-picking over details. Accuracy is always commendable, but perfection is sometimes unattainable when the urgent requirement is to meet a deadline.

HOW TO COPE

1 There are no shortcuts. You have to do your homework. The only way to beat experts is to out-expert them.

2 When you do have the facts at your fingertips, it's difficult to challenge directly their expertise, they'll always have an answer. Try a gentle alternative viewpoint that doesn't undermine them.

3 Let them know you appreciate their expertise by listening actively and acknowledging their knowledge. Everyone likes to feel that their opinion counts. By being seen to take on board what you are being told, you gain useful leverage in expecting that your views be listened to as well.

Know-it-all expert continued

4 Listen actively and acknowledge. Paraphrase rather than interrupt; it shows you respect their expertise. Their egos demand recognition.

5 If you come across mistakes in their arguments, ask them for clarification with a seemingly innocuous question. They'll take pride in going away and finding out the correct answer, and that can only be valuable in the long run for your team.

6 Never correct them in front of others—not unless you want to be in the middle of a public argument that you could end up losing.

7 If you are suggesting a solution that differs from theirs, try and make them feel they are part of the decision making. Use phrases like: "What do you think about x" and "Should we try this?"

8 Go back to point one. Never skimp on preparation.

Arrogance

HOW TO RECOGNIZE

- You may feel small in the face of their self-importance.

- They'll make no bones about showing that they are the best.

- They have a way of intimidating others not to challenge their sense of superiority.

- They try to draw attention to themselves. There is nothing worse for them than to feel ignored.

- They can be very critical and judgmental of others.

- They rarely listen to others and react to events based on their own preconceptions rather than the facts.

- They never take the blame.

HOW TO COPE

1 Avoid putting them down in front of co-workers. They won't forgive you. Arrange a meeting in private instead.

2 Remind them they are part of a team and that a team thrives on cooperation.

3 If you are going to criticize them, give them some praise first.

4 Even when they are their most aloof, respond with a friendly, warm manner. You don't want to appear arrogant yourself.

5 You can't compliment them (if they deserve it) enough. Their arrogance may shield insecurity. Showing them appreciation will make them feel more confident and a valuable asset to the team.

Impatience

HOW TO RECOGNIZE

- They tend to be very pushy.

- They also make unreasonable demands. When a manager wants a job done "by yesterday" and this is plainly unrealistic, employees feel harassed and make mistakes or take a longer time in resistance.

- They never work in the present. They are always thinking of the next deadline and can't enjoy their current job.

- They tend to take more work than they can handle, are late to meetings, and miss deadlines.

HOW TO COPE

1 You shouldn't allow yourself to be bullied into working at their pace. If they are in a hurry, ask them to slow down.

2 Don't worry about reminding them that there is plenty of time to do whatever is needed.

3 Fight with reason. Tell them you would like to work at their pace but that you want to do a decent job and that you need extra time.

4 If they seem anxious about their future assignments, help them by suggesting changes to their timetable.

5 Ask them to repeat themselves. This can help buy you time by putting the brakes on.

Obstinacy

HOW TO RECOGNIZE

- They resist changes.

- They don't seem to listen to other's opinions.

- They stall on giving answers.

- When rushed or pushed, they will get angry and dig their heels in deeper.

- They avoid decisions and delay projects that need to be completed.

HOW TO COPE

1 Communicate better: Explain to them the changes that they are fearful of. Don't just assume they understand them.

2 Give them time to adjust to whatever is changing. Whatever you do, don't surprise them.

3 Don't make sudden demands.

4 Encourage them to feel they have options. Their stubbornness may be their response to a feeling that you are trying to control them.

5 Don't give orders. Ask them for input on issues.

Self-deprecation

HOW TO RECOGNIZE

- They are embarrassed when you signal them out, whether it's for criticism or praise.

- They won't volunteer for tasks or assignments even though they are suitable candidates.

- They always blame themselves or put themselves down.

- They start to appear defensive and apologetic.

- They don't take their share of team responsibility.

HOW TO COPE

1 Give them time to adjust to whatever is changing. Whatever you do, don't surprise them.

2 Let them know when they've done a good job. They are likely to balk at praise. Tell them you mean it. This encourages positive thinking on their part.

3 Don't make up praise. Their tendency to put themselves down will only lead them to disbelief. Try and back praise with examples.

4 Try not to put too much pressure on them in front of others.

Self-destruction

HOW TO RECOGNIZE

- They make decisions knowing that the result will be a negative one.

- They appear to be consuming too much alcohol or are abusing other substances.

- They are frequently unwell.

- They miss several consecutive deadlines.

- They stop taking care of their personal appearance.

HOW TO COPE

1 Be alert to any signs of self-destruction: binge drinking, excessive smoking.

2 Never cover up for them or hide their absence or drunken behavior.

3 If you are the manager, let them know that you will take disciplinary action if their self-destructive behavior continues.

4 Try talking to them about their problem. They may resist, and you are unlikely to be able to change their behavior. But at least you have let them know you know they have a problem. This makes it easier to take drastic action later.

dealing with difficult types & behaviors

Martyrdom

HOW TO RECOGNIZE

- They appear dissatisfied or unhappy.

- They often have a whiney tone that irritates co-workers.

- They tend to complain a lot.

- They seem to suffer a lot of mishaps and feel compelled to tell you about them.

HOW TO COPE

1 Don't volunteer them for extra work. They will be eager to take it on and even more eager to let you know how much work they have.

2 Don't let them get away with their mournful accounts of unending problems and bad luck. Ask them in a matter of fact way to detail exactly how luck played a part in their crises. Let them see that they may be responsible for their own actions.

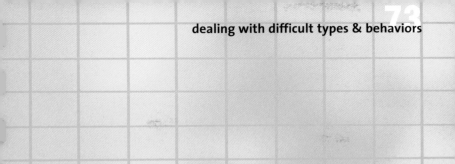

3 If their complaints continue, suggest they go to see the relevant supervisor or manager to sort the problem out.

4 Try not to indulge their complaints in order just to sidetrack them. Don't agree that life is terrible and nothing but a series of injustices. Be polite, but point out that for every hard luck story there is one where people have successfully battled through.

dealing with difficult types & behaviors

Sniping

HOW TO REGOGNIZE

■ They don't like direct confrontations. They prefer to make criticisms through sneaky, sarcastic remarks. Look out for an exaggerated roll of the eyes, a biting tone, or an underhand remark.

■ Their ability to put others down makes them poor team players.

■ They like stirring up trouble.

■ They like to make people laugh with their interventions as a way of raising their self-esteem.

HOW TO COPE

1 Bring them out of hiding. For instance at a meeting, if they come up with a snide remark, don't overlook it. Ask them to repeat it. Use a phrase like: "Excuse me, what is your exact point? Would you like to share it with the rest of us?" The chances are they'll be slightly more embarrassed to repeat their remarks. Their potshots are never as effective a second time around.

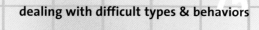
2 Don't be amused by their intervention. Take any comment very seriously.

3 If they deny having made a remark, ask others to verify that they heard them. It will make them think twice before making future interventions.

4 Take the sniper aside and suggest a meeting. Say you take his comments seriously and would appreciate it if he spelled out his grievances. He is far less likely to resort to humor and sarcasm when you set a serious tone.

dealing with difficult types & behaviors

Anger

HOW TO RECOGNIZE

■ They appear tense or frustrated.

■ They blow up easily.

■ They lose emotional control.

■ They start shouting.

HOW TO COPE

1 Aim to defuse the anger rather than confront the individual, which will make the situation worse.

2 Try to get yourself heard while they are blowing up. Call their names, signal with a hand, but don't shout over their voices.

3 Sympathize with them. Show them that you are paying attention. Use a phrase like: "I can see you are very upset right now. Maybe we can talk about this a bit later?"

4 Remain calm. Although it is tempting to tell them what you think of their behavior, you will only raise the temperature further if you join in.

5 If anger persists, point out that it is a damaging emotion. Anger manifests itself as aggressiveness, which is offputting for others to have to deal with in the workplace.

Indecision

HOW TO RECOGNIZE

- They don't know what they really want .

- They don't have the confidence to make a decision.

- They need to discuss decisions with others.

- They prefer oral information and don't want to be pinned down to a written agreement, which cannot be changed. They would like the option of changing their minds.

- They keep putting off any course of action until it is too late.

HOW TO COPE

1 Don't put them in charge of any project that involves deadlines or timely deliverables.

2 You can't intimidate or hurry them into making a decision. That will only make them feel nervous, and their natural response will be to postpone any decision.

3 Praise a job well done to encourage them into having more confidence in their judgment. Reassure them that they can do a good job.

4 Let them know the importance of prioritizing. That should help them make up their minds what issues are worth mulling over and what they shouldn't be thinking about too much.

5 Try to assign them to a minor task that entails speedy decisions. There's nothing like training to boost confidence.

6 Encourage them to use a decision-making system such as writing down the pros and cons of a certain course of action. A system that they can turn to every time they have to come to a conclusion can aid decision making.

3

confronting difficult behavior

Considering your options

Once you are fully aware of the different varieties of difficult behavior and how they recur in different guises in the workplace, you face the challenge of how to respond. To gain short-term peace, you may decide to live with the problematic behavior. Leaving a problem unaddressed may only make the situation worse. Below are the three basic ways in which managers respond to difficult behavior:

1 DENIAL

You can choose to ignore the situation. Looking the other way may appear to be an easy option in the short-term. You may fear that confronting the situation will only intensify the conflict. You may chose to pretend not to notice the poor behavior to preserve harmony within a team.

Ultimately though, indifference to problematic behavior may only encourage the individual to worsen her behavior, especially if the person is choosing to be difficult to draw attention to herself. Also, the longer you put off confronting the problem, the worse it is likely to get. Your state of denial might include anger or resentment at having to interrupt your normal activities to handle the situation. Beware that taking no action will mean going through life getting upset each time you have to deal with this person.

2 ACCEPTANCE

You may weigh up the pros and cons of the situation and decide that it's far better to keep the peace and simply learn to live with the difficult person. But this response could backfire with the problem person because he will react to your passive behavior and continue to goad you further into some action. Whatever aspects of the difficult person annoyed you in the first place are likely to continue niggling at you unless the person has substantially changed his behavior. You could end up spending a lot of your precious time and energy trying to put up with a situation you find unsatisfactory deep down, when you could be tackling the problem in a more productive manner. This is the point when you accept that the difficult behavior deserves an active response. Alternatively, you can look at your own standards and behavior and evaluate whether you can modify these to put up with what you perceive as difficult behavior in another person.

Considering your options continued

3 CONFRONTATION

You can take the most challenging route of facing the difficult behavior head-on. That does not mean matching aggressive, angry behavior with similar hostility. It means sitting back calmly, assessing your options, and planning an assertive course of action. Usually you take this path when you realize that you only have power over your actions, not that of others. It's up to you to try to change your response to a problem person. You can even turn the situation around and ask yourself how you would feel if you were in this person's shoes. Ask the problem person why she acts as she does and try to make sense of it. Put yourself in her place and treat her as you would like to be treated.

4 A COMBINATION OF ALL THREE

You will be tempted to veer from one approach to another, depending on how you are feeling at any given point, and what the circumstances are. Some days you will feel proactive and will want to get involved in dealing with a problem. Other days, you may feel there are more important issues to deal with and so assume the problem will sort itself out. Be careful though—to deal with people effectively, consistency is important. You will influence people's behavior if they know that you are bound to react in a certain way. This does not mean that you should apply an identical formula to every situation; just realize that if you are constantly changing, it may be your behavior that becomes part of the problem.

Pinpointing problem behavior

Once you have made the decision to confront the difficult person, it is useful before taking any further action, to write down the exact problem. The following are some tips on what to think about.

1
AVOID GENERALITIES OR PERSONAL ATTACKS
These tend to be seen as too vague and open for misinterpretation. The person can also mistake it as a personal attack on his personality.

Phrases not to use:

"Every time you are at a meeting, your very presence causes problems."

"I can't remember the last time you weren't sarcastic about something."

"Everyone agrees that you're a trouble maker."

2 BE SPECIFIC

The clearer and more focused your observations, the easier it is for the person to understand exactly what it is about her behavior, rather than her personality, that is at the root of the complaint.

Phrases to use:

"Your intervention at the middle of the meeting [show her the written minutes] was unhelpful because we had already discussed that with you."

"Can you see how your sarcastic comment about the new project could have caused offense?"

"Your refusal to participate yesterday caused unnecessary trouble for others."

3 DOUBLE CHECK

Return to your notes a day or two later and see if your observations were justified. That way you can check that your own anger or frustration didn't color your point of view. If necessary, show your comments to a trusted colleague who isn't involved in the situation. It's difficult sometimes to view a problem objectively on your own.

Arranging a meeting

When you are persuaded that your grievances with the problem person are justified and that you have ample evidence to back your arguments, the next step is to arrange a meeting with the difficult party.

PUBLIC FACE-OFF
In rare situations, confronting difficult people's behavior in public is an appropriate option especially if they have deliberately chosen to be difficult in a public arena.

TIPS

1

Make sure your public intervention is assertive and concise. Move swiftly on after making your point. The last thing you want is to make it seem to be a point-scoring session where you come out the winner, and the difficult person, the humiliated loser. This will only force the difficult person to adopt even more extreme behavior.

2

Gentle humor or sarcasm sometimes work.

PRIVATE INTERVIEW
The safest option by far is to arrange a private meeting where there are fewer chances for the difficult person to feel he is being picked on in front of others. You also avoid any surprises or unexpected interventions from colleagues.

TIPS

1 Try not to meet with the employee too soon after the difficult incident as emotions on both sides are likely to be running high.

2 Don't postpone the meeting for too long either. A couple of days is best, but don't let it take longer than a week.

Arranging a meeting continued

3 If you anticipate the person is going to be abusive, ask someone from human resources to join the meeting. In a smaller company, you may have no choice but to handle the person alone.

4 Give a brief explanation for the meeting but don't go into detail. The time for discussion is at the meeting, not before.

5 Put the request for a meeting in writing if possible. A record of the procedure will help later on if the situation gets heated and there is no cooperation from the difficult people. For instance, they might try to shirk away from the meeting.

6 Read up on employee law if you are in a small company. If you are in a big company, you should be able to get some legal advice quickly.

7 Get all the parties to agree on the minutes, sign and date what was discussed and agreed.

8 If necessary draw up an agenda beforehand. This will help steer the meeting in the right direction, help stop it from derailing at awkward moments, and help you time the meeting so you cover all the points you need to discuss. Where possible, get agreement from the other person before the meeting on the agenda items.

confronting difficult behavior

Effective listening

During a meeting with difficult people, effective listening is key to a successful outcome. The key qualities for effective listening are patience, focus, and understanding. Encouraging an individual to discuss her issues without appearing condescending or judgmental will greatly increase your chances of finding an eventual solution. If a problem person genuinely believes you are trying sincerely to solve her problem, then the individual is far more likely to respond positively. On the other hand, poor listening leads to misunderstandings.

BLOCKS TO EFFECTIVE LISTENING

1
You are more concerned about what you are going to say next than what the speaker is telling you.

2
You are too busy arguing internally with the speaker to embrace what she is saying. This means that you cannot really listen—too much of your attention is taken up with knee-jerk reactions that occur on a minute-by-minute basis.

3 You have too many preconceptions about the speaker so you think you know what the speaker is saying.

4 You have allocated only a limited time for the meeting, and the speaker is rambling incoherently or repeating old grievances you've heard before.

5 You are allowing phone calls to interrupt the flow of the meeting.

Effective listening continued

WHAT DOES POOR LISTENING SAY ABOUT YOU?

1 You are anxious, and this makes you a nervous chatterer who pays little attention to others.

2 You are opinionated and so concerned with putting your points across that others are unable to express their opinions.

3 You are close-minded and feel threatened by any new opinions or points of view.

4 You are shy and too worried about what the person is thinking about you to be listening properly.

HOW TO BECOME A BETTER LISTENER

1 Try to imagine you are meeting the person for the first time.

2 Remember that people love expressing their opinions and that they are flattered when someone pays them attention. They are more likely to respond favorably to you if you give them some time.

3 Block out other thoughts during the meeting and focus closely on the matter at hand. After all, you want to find a solution.

4 Sit quietly and attentively. Fidgeting, shuffling your notes, or picking pieces of fluff off your suit are all signs that your attention is elsewhere.

Effective listening continued

5 Look and sound like you're listening. Tilt your head forward; nod to show that you are paying attention. Just the act of pretending you are listening is concentrating your mind, and you will automatically be listening more carefully.

6 Avoid interrupting if you are not asking a question.

7 If the person is rambling, try to hold on to key words and phrases.

8 If the person is angry, allow her to let off steam. Don't try to calm her down. This will only make her angrier.

9 Don't fold your arms. This expresses resistance.

10 Avoid showing you may not be following the conversation unless you are totally lost. Don't give any puzzled looks or show disagreement.

Effective listening continued

PRACTICAL TIPS

1

TAKE NOTES
You don't need to jot down every word, which looks rude. You also want to make lots of eye contact to show you are engaged with the speaker. Jotting down key words or phrases at specific moments shows you are emphasizing what the speaker is saying. It's also helpful for you for future feedback.

2

PARAPHRASE
This is an excellent tool to show you are alert to the speaker's train of thought and that you understand. It is also very useful to repeat phrases that you might not have quite understood. It's equally a test of the speaker's own listening tools. If the speaker responds, "No, that's not what I really mean," then you know that he's listening to you, and it also clears up any misunderstanding on your part. Also referred to as backtracking, this form of feedback is particularly important when dealing with people on the phone where you don't have many clues about the person's nonverbal behavior.

3 CLARIFY

At this stage, you don't need to come up with any answers. You are still on an information-gathering exercise so keep asking questions that show you are trying to get to the bottom of what you are being told. If the person is excitable, it forces him to give rational answers. A person who is giving vague generalizations is also forced to be specific.

4 SUMMARIZE

At the end, summarize what has been said in order to make sure you fully understand what has been agreed throughout the course of the meeting. This is also a useful tool for gently stating the areas that need further attention. The final benefit is that any misconceptions or areas where a misunderstanding might arise can be cleared up right away. This prevents potentially tense situations from developing later on where you have to haggle over exactly who said what to whom, or what was really meant by what was said.

confronting difficult behavior

Effective speaking

A vital communication skill, complementary to effective listening, is being able to put your point across succinctly. However, like poor listening, there are blocks to effective speaking that you must recognize before being able to move forward.

BLOCKS TO EFFECTIVE SPEAKING

1 You don't articulate clearly.

2 You haven't written down points properly so there's no logic or order in your speech.

3 You use long-winded sentences.

4 You are unclear about what you want from your listener.

5 You raise your tone of voice to try to sound authoritative. Listeners switch off.

6 You fail to notice if the listener has tuned out.

WHAT DOES POOR SPEAKING SAY ABOUT YOU?

1 You are unsure and hesitant.

2 You are nervous and uptight.

3 You have little confidence in the meeting.

4 You show little commitment to resolving the problem.

confronting difficult behavior

Effective speaking continued

HOW TO BECOME A BETTER SPEAKER

1 Listen to your own voice as if you were the listener. Are you being clear?

2 Take appropriate pauses to allow the listener to consider what you are saying.

3 Make sure you are not talking too loudly or too quietly.

4 Take some notes with you and check to make sure that you have covered all your main points.

5 Practice speaking into a tape recorder and playing it back. Analyze how you could say the same thing using more precise language.

6 Make sure your body language reinforces what you are saying and be alert to the tone of your voice.

PRACTICAL TIPS

1 Put yourself in the listener's position. Are you being clear?

2 Avoid "you" language such as "you should" or "you must." Use "I" language instead like "I was expecting" or "I encourage you to...."

3 Use specific examples of difficult behavior: "Remember last Monday before the meeting..." rather than "As usual, you sabotaged...."

4 Avoid phrases that trigger difficult and defensive behavior: "It's company policy"; "I want you to"; "You have to"; "I need you to."

5 Remember to use the listener's name.

confronting difficult behavior

Interpreting nonverbal signals

People can reveal as much about themselves through body language as through speech. People's posture or tone of voice can often contradict what they are saying. For instance, they may be apologizing for a mistake, but their body language conveys frustration and annoyance. Don't underestimate the extent to which people listen with their eyes. It's essential for you to pick up on nonverbal signals.

SOME EXAMPLES OF BODY LANGUAGE THAT CAN TELL US ABOUT A PERSON:

1 Clenched jaw: the person is angry or upset.

2 Frowning: the person is in disagreement or confused.

3 Dropped shoulders: the person is depressed or tired.

4 Flushed face: the person could have high blood pressure, but it's more likely that he's angry or embarrassed.

5 Nose or head scratching: the person is uncomfortable about what she's saying or she may be lying.

6 Finger tapping: the person is impatient or nervous.

7 Folded arms: the person is on the defensive.

8 Frenetic body movements: the person is nervous.

9 An open posture: the person appears to be friendly and open.

10 Chest and chin down: this position discourages dialog.

11 Sitting rigidly behind your desk: this position can appear confrontational. It's better to sit perpendicular to the person.

Blending

People get on best with others when they share common ground. When the differences between two people far outweigh the similarities, there is a far greater opportunity for conflict. An essential communication skill that encourages people to establish a rapport, even if they are coming from very different position, is blending. There are several ways of blending, which is another way of describing the various things people do to try to find things in common to further positive interaction.

1

BLENDING USING FACIAL AND BODY EXPRESSIONS
People often remark that a couple or a pair of close siblings tend to have similar facial expression, body posture, and ways of moving their hands. That's because they spend a lot of time together and end up mirroring each other, revealing they are comfortable with each other. Copying each other's body and facial expression is a way of complementing one another. For instance, when you watch two angry people, notice that they are both raising their hands at each other or clenching their fists. Conversely, you can notice that a meeting is going well when the participants are smiling at each other and mimicking their gestures unconsciously.

2 BLENDING VOCALLY

People have different ways of talking, but when a relationship is deepening and the participants have respect and liking for each other, it is likely that they will start blending vocally. The faster speaker may try to slow down, and the slow talker will try to speed up. A quiet person may try talking louder to a noisy person, and a loud person may turn down the volume. Whatever way around it works, both people gradually enter into a vocal rapport where they mirror each other's way of communicating.

confronting difficult behavior

Keeping positive

Helping the person feel worthwhile and showing her that you are seeking resolution, not punishment, creates a warm glow during the meeting that is more likely to bear positive results.

CREATING POSITIVES

1 If you are angry about something, don't show it. Just relate your anger in a calm way. It will make you look in control. Try to imagine that the aggrieved party is someone else.

2 Ask questions about the person's behavior. Allow her to explain herself, but don't make her defensive.

3 Avoid interrupting. Let the other person have a chance to say what she thinks. Only by really listening to her answers without interruption will you be able to have a constructive conversation. You will find out things you may have overlooked or have your assumptions dispelled.

4 Try to match the person's body language. Mirroring suggests empathy. It's not a sign that you are agreeing, just that you accept what the person is saying and feeling. When the individual starts mirroring you back, it means you've encouraged a more positive attitude.

5 If you are delivering some harsh news or disciplinary action, share your logic. For instance, don't just say, "You have to improve." Help her think she has a choice.

"I want you to improve, and I think this system will help you succeed. It's up to you how you behave. I'll reward improvements in the following way."

6 Explore alternatives. By offering suggestions about what you can do, you keep the conversation on a positive plane. You might find that what is settled for is less than you imagined.

Keeping positive continued

By contrast, there are several things you should not do if you want to avoid putting a negative spin on the meeting. Negativity hampers manager's efforts to improve effective communication.

ELIMINATING NEGATIVES

The last thing you want during a meeting is to dampen the atmosphere. The following situations create a hostile environment.

1 Arriving late to the meeting.

2 Failing to shake the difficult person's hand or to offer them a chair.

3 Accepting calls or emails during the meeting.

4 Using a brisk, harsh tone that suggests you are reprimanding them.

5 Making blunt, opening statements that show you've already made up your mind about the course of action you are going to take.

Effective negotiation

The best negotiations are when both parties feel they have come out winning. This involves an open dialog and a search for a mutually beneficial goal. It is far more common though for people to view negotiations as a tug of war. The following are steps for transforming conflict into co-operation.

1

BECOME A PEACEMAKER
Decide what lengths you are prepared to go to make peace with the other person and how much a resolution is worth to your company and your prospects. If your answer is positive, then approach the person for a meeting. Let him know you are making the overture as a peacemaker and that you assume he wants to resolve the problem.

Assuming this role will help the other person look at you in a more moderate, favorable light. You will appear as someone who genuinely wants reconciliation rather than someone who simply wants to impose a settlement or dominate the relationship. You will appear as someone who is not trying to be judge and executioner.

2   PINPOINT THE PROBLEM
Write down the problem to confront and what objectives you expect to achieve after meeting with the person.

Examples of problems to face are:

"Mary continues to be late for work in spite of several warnings about timekeeping."

"Joe is affecting office morale and causing me stress with his constant whining"

Once you have detailed the specific name or identified the problem, write down your goals for the meeting. Examples:

"Mary has to come in to work on time."

"Joe must stop complaining, or I'll have to move him to another location."

Effective negotiation continued

3 WRITE POSSIBLE OBJECTIONS
Put yourself in the shoes of your problem employee and other colleagues. What objections, reactions, or disagreements may he have in a potential meeting. What are the three main points you fear he may bring up during the meeting. Do you have answers to these concerns? Try to work out a solution for each concern. Writing these fears down on paper should help to reduce their impact on you.

4 ORGANIZE YOUR NOTES
It is preferable to have as much ammunition or evidence as possible to draw upon during a potentially fiery face-off. Track down any other supporting documents.

5 MEET IN PRIVATE
However tempting it may be to raise some of your concerns with a bigger audience that might support you, arrange the meeting where you will not be disturbed. Make it a space that you control.

Effective negotiation continued

AT THE MEETING

1 Explain the specific problem you wish to resolve by a certain date not too far in the future.

2 Look the person clearly in the eye as you establish the boundaries for the discussion.

3 Invite him to ask any questions or make any suggestions to your ultimate goals. This is very important. Everyone likes to be heard and feel that their opinion and point of view is being taken seriously and incorporated into any plan. Listen quietly and without interruption while he is speaking.

4 If the difficult person cannot agree with any of your objectives, you have to be flexible with your goals and try to identify what common goal you can agree on. What may at first appear as a stalemate could be turned to a situation of mutual cooperation if you ask enough questions. Listen carefully to the other person and make certain he feels understood.

5 Paraphrase the person's position, and if it differs considerably from yours, repeat your list of points and underline which ones you are flexible with and which are nonnegotiable. Do your homework and try to imagine what the list of the person's objections will be. That way you won't be too caught by surprise, and you can prepare a counteroffer. Remain objective and judge whether the person's grievances have any substance.

Effective negotiation continued

6 Acknowledge any grievances. Repeat his complaints back to him.

7 Sometimes you have to agree to disagree on any sticking point. Coming to that conclusion is in itself a step forward because at least both parties seem to be approaching the same conclusion.

8 Try instead to find points of agreement and underline them.

9 Paraphrase agreed terms to emphasize understanding.

10 Set a realistic timeframe to achieve mutually agreed upon goals.

11 Don't be afraid to say "no." Don't give a long list of reasons for your decision.

12 Establish some boundaries for yourself. Know what you are going to be able to put up with. You may want to communicate those boundaries or you may not, depending on the situation.

13 If you fail to agree on anything, try to keep the lines of communication open for future dialog.

14 In the event of some sort of agreement, confirm this in writing. This is important because it clearly spells out what has been agreed to. Send the other person the document and ask for comments or amendments. This input will help ensure that the agreement is adhered to.

SOME PITFALLS TO AVOID

1 Don't act passively during a meeting and admit defeat.

2 Don't disregard the wishes of the difficult person for the sake of personal victory.

3 Don't avoid any sort of outcome so that neither party wins.

4 Don't fail to take down notes and establish mutual goals.

AFTER THE MEETING

It is crucial to write a summary of the meeting with the main points discussed. It is also useful to set up a timeframe to put the agreed upon changes into effect.

You could also write a more celebratory note congratulating the person on having reached an agreement. Explain how a swift resolution has helped the company.

WHEN IT ALL GOES WRONG

Sometimes there are no satisfactory conclusions to a meeting. The options open are:

1 Call in a mediator. This could be a senior colleague or an external mediator or consultant. Make sure the chosen person is trusted by both parties.

2 The worst possible scenario is that even a mediator fails to broker any sort of deal. You may decide to cut your losses and limit the difficult person's access to you. Choose projects the difficult person is not involved with.

Effective negotiation continued

3 Avoidance is not always an option. You could possibly request that the difficult person be transferred to another job.

4 If there are no vacancies, you may have no other choice but to leave your job. Do this once you've weighed up all the pros and cons of staying or moving on.

5 If you decide to stay on, you must decide to draw a line on resolving differences with the problem colleague and move on.

6 Once you've decided that changing jobs is the only option, pause and think before storming into your boss's office with a dramatic resignation. At this stage, you only want to put your job search into action. As with all stages of dealing with difficult people, try to remain calm, think clearly, and take one step at a time. Speedy resignations are almost always regretted—you will be the one losing your livelihood.

7   Start to approach potential employers; start actively seeking old colleagues out. Update your resume and obtain some decent references. That way, if a new job interview comes up, you are ready to act.

REVIEW YOUR PERFORMANCE

Try to answer a few questions about your performance to gauge your level of success:

1   Did we come up with an action plan that can be realistically reviewed in a few months' time?

2   Did I listen carefully to the objections raised?

3   Did I define the problem and present options to solve it?

4

dealing with difficult bosses

Are you a difficult employee?

One of the leading reasons for job dissatisfaction is a difficult boss. It is commonly said that people don't leave jobs, they leave difficult supervisors. But bosses can be useful scapegoats for an employee's own set of failings and insecurities. That's why putting yourself in the boss's shoes is a good way of looking objectively at the boss-employee relationship.

CONSIDER

1 Do you think that your boss doesn't give you enough guidance, but are you slow at following instructions? Do you expect to be spoon fed? Are you needy?

2 Do you dislike taking orders? Do you wish you were the boss? Are you in a realistic position to be the boss?

3 Do other co-workers complain about your boss? If they do, do they have the same grievances?

4 Have you had similar problems with other bosses?

5 Are you sure it isn't a question of chemistry? You're an extrovert and she's an introvert. Your boss likes an early start. You don't mind staying on later during the evenings. Simply, you like doing things in different ways.

6 Have you tried to see the situation from your boss's point of view? Are there any reasons why your boss would be unhappy with your performance?

dealing with difficult bosses

Do you hate being criticized by the boss?

Bosses can be notoriously poor at giving positive guidance. But employees can also be too quick to perceive a justifiable correction as negative criticism. Employees need to learn to take critcism in a positive way.

TIPS

1 Be open to the boss's suggestions. Don't be thinking of how you are going to defend yourself. You may miss some valid constructive points.

2 If you feel the criticism is vague, try to draw your boss into specifics. Focusing on a particular episode makes it easier for both of you to have a discussion that doesn't descend into a personal argument.

3 Paraphrase the boss's criticism back to make sure you have understood all the points.

4 Bosses are there to criticize and try to improve employees' performance. Don't take it personally, decide not to repeat the same mistake, and move on.

The boss as a client

It may help to see your boss as a customer who is paying for your services. This may be difficult to swallow, but there's no escaping the fact that pleasing your boss is one of the main ways of getting ahead in your career. The boss is the main person responsible for your raises, your performance, and your chances of promotion. Even if you want to move on, your boss will have to be your referee. The following are some basic ways of keeping a boss satisfied.

1
RESPECT YOUR BOSS'S TIME
Remember that your boss is probably juggling various projects and people at the same time. You can't always be in his mind. If the boss doesn't seem to have taken any notice of you lately, it could be due to a heavy workload. Your boss will appreciate any communication with him to be direct and concise. Don't worry. If your boss wants more details, he won't hesitate to ask for them.

2 GRAB YOUR BOSS'S ATTENTION
Your boss's time may be precious, but sometimes there is no alternative but to demand your boss's undivided attention. Don't just burst into your boss's office demanding an immediate interview. It is far better to schedule an appointment. Suggest a venue outside his room if you really want no distractions or interruptions. Let the boss know how important this time, however brief, is for you. The boss can't guess that you need his time.

3 FULFILL YOUR END OF THE BARGAIN
In the same way that the boss has a duty to supervise you effectively, you have certain responsibilities toward your boss, such as sticking to deadlines, alerting him to any problems or delays ahead of time, and of accepting blame for your mistakes.

Types of difficult bosses

After careful consideration, your conclusion is still that your boss, not you, is the problem. Here is an overview of the common types of difficult bosses, their motivations, and strategies for dealing with them.

OVERVIEW

1 Aggressive boss

2 Hands-on boss

3 Hands-off boss

4 Weak, inexperienced boss

Managers, too, might recognize themselves in these descriptions. They should answer some of the questions opposite as honestly as possible, and see what the results are.

QUESTIONS FOR BOSSES

1 How would you classify your style of management?

2 Do you expect your employees to work as hard as you do?

3 How much room do you give employees for original thinking?

4 Do you expect workers to follow your rules?

5 Do you make sure you and your staff take all their holidays?

6 Do you believe in rewarding employees?

7 Have you ever asked an employee how she felt about her job?

Aggressive boss

One of the most common types of bosses that create problems in the workplace use aggression to force their way around. They believe that bullying people achieves best results, maybe because they fear appearing soft or perhaps because they are repeating the behavior they received from former aggressive bosses.

HOW IT AFFECTS YOU

1

TEMPER TANTRUMS
Bosses who have tantrums on a regular basis may think it's a normal way of behaving. They may have picked this up from watching too many bad films featuring over-the-top business moguls. The fact is that the vision of adults having what amounts to a hissy fit can be laughable at best, threatening at worst. Don't respond with anger. They will be too busy fuming to notice you anyway. You could try imagining the boss as a naughty toddler throwing toys on the floor. Alternatively, you could take no notice at all. That may discourage a repeat performance.

2 SILENT TREATMENT

A boss ignoring an employee for sometimes days after an incident that didn't go his way is an undignified but all too common ploy used by bosses. It appears like a passive action, but the boss is definitely trying to punish a colleague. Try to show you haven't noticed the boss isn't talking to you and initiate conversations regardless. Even try: "I assume as you haven't said anything to the contrary, that you want me to continue with the approach I suggested." If that isn't what he wants to hear, you can bet the silent treatment will be over, and he'll think twice before using that strategy again.

Aggressive boss continued

3 SEXUAL HARASSMENT

The growing number of cases of sexual harassment may prevent some managers from attempting unsolicited sexual advances, mainly to women, but don't count on it. Managers, particularly male managers, have practiced this type of aggression for years. Harassment doesn't have to be physical necessarily. It can take the form of leering remarks about what you're wearing; inappropriate jokes are also a form of aggression. Try to take notes of when they have occurred and keep a record. Try to get other co-workers who have witnessed these incidents to corroborate that what you consider harassment isn't in your imagination. Ask them if they would support you in the event of your taking the case to human resources or a lawyer.

4 SARCASM

Sarcasm isn't only the lowest form of wit; it is rather a nasty method of trying to put a person down. However difficult, try not to rise to the bait. The sarcastic boss wants you either to respond by defending yourself or to show you're hurt.

One response is to pretend to take the sarcastic remark very literally and to ask the boss to elaborate. The manager may be too taken aback to respond with further sarcasm.

Aggressive boss continued

HOW TO REACT

1 Find some allies, preferably in superior positions. You might need the support later on if things get really sticky.

2 Don't go to war in public. As the boss, she will expect to win.

3 You can attempt arranging a meeting with the aggressive boss to let her know the impact that her actions or words are having on you or your performance. She might be surprised to know how you feel.

4 At the meeting, don't make generalizations about her personality. It's far better to focus on specific examples of behavior and explain how it makes you feel.

5 Help the boss save face. Don't let her think she hasn't been observant. Pick phrases like: "You are probably unaware..." or "I'm sure you didn't intend...."

6 When a boss that works long hours expects you to do the same, point out that you need a realistic work/life balance or your work will suffer.

Aggressive boss continued

7 If the boss responds aggressively, firmly but calmly tell her you find her behavior is unfair and that you don't expect to be treated in this way.

8 In the event that the boss does suggest she will work on certain points, try to hold him to her commitments. One way of doing this is following up the meeting with a letter or email outlining the results of the meeting.

9 When the boss refuses to acknowledge her aggressive behavior, you could appeal to her own boss and to human resources. Try to make a couple of objective points that you can back up with concrete evidence. Don't make it personal. Be prepared to wait some time to see any results.

10 Sometimes you just have to accept that the boss is unable to change or that nobody above her is committed to forcing a change. One option is to ask for a transfer to another department.

11 A space in another department may not be available. You have no choice left but to search for a new job. Conduct your job search as secretly as possible. You will have to think very carefully about asking your manager for a reference. You'll also have to decide how much of the boss's behavior you will want to discuss in any potential interview. The last thing you want to let an employer know is that you face problems with people at work. They may assume you have the problem, not your boss.

Hands-on boss

The biggest potential problem with hands-on managers is that they provide a little too much direction. They are scared to let go of any responsibilities. This is usually attributable to their insecurity and not any reflection on your abilities. Alternatively, they may not want to share the limelight with you.

HOW IT AFFECTS YOU

1 It doesn't matter how much detail you provide the boss or how many times you check a piece of work, it's never right. You are likely to feel unappreciated. Why won't the boss trust you and give you more independence?

2 You could also feel bored. If the boss is reluctant to delegate, then you will lack motivation to improve. There is little room to move up either with such a controlling manager.

3 Your boss is so absorbed in his own role and how he can run all parts of the business himself that there is hardly any opportunity for you to test your own ideas out. The boss is simply not interested in encouraging any input from you even though you may have been working in a specific area longer than he has.

4 You could also feel trapped by the lack of chances to gain new skills. A boss who is supervising your work so heavily is hardly going to be confident about you expanding your horizons.

Hands-on boss continued

HOW TO REACT

1 Let the boss know gently that you appreciate the concern but that you don't want to bother him with extra work. The boss might be relieved that you are showing initiative.

2 With the boss's anxiety in mind, anticipate issues before handing in work, and take extra care to show that you have covered all the bases. The reassurance may encourage future trust. Try a phrase like: "I would like you to trust my performance so you have more time to spend on other important issues."

3 Surprise the boss by completing an assignment before he has become involved with it. If he's been lacking confidence in delegating work, it may prove a watershed for him to see you have coped perfectly well by yourself.

4 Inform him of your objectives. A busy boss can't guess where your future ambitions lie. At this point it is up to you to say where you would like your career path to go, and the parts of your work that interest you the most.

5 If the boss is deliberately holding you back due to a fear of competition, make sure other directors know about it.

dealing with difficult bosses

Hands-off boss

An invisible manager may appeal to the few employees who are genuinely self-sufficient, but what about the majority of workers who need direction and crave feedback?

HOW IT AFFECTS YOU

1 A manager who is hands-off may have too much on his own plate. He may feel overwhelmed with responsibilities. Such self-absorption leaves a team feeling rudderless.

2 You feel unappreciated. It seems to make no difference to the boss how you are performing.

3 If you're feeling insecure about your work or are facing particular problems, there's no one to turn to.

4 You worry about future promotions. Does the boss ever notice what you've accomplished?

HOW TO REACT

1 Take the initiative to write down what you want to achieve and make a copy for the boss. It makes it more difficult to plead indifference if you've put your thoughts down on paper.

2 Pin your boss down by email to a suggested meeting time.

3 During the meeting, be sensitive to the boss's lack of time, which is causing the problem in the first place. Stick to the critical issues. Make sure these are clear to him and cover yourself by confirming any agreement in writing.

4 Provide your own milestones and evaluate your effectiveness in meeting them at regular intervals.

Weak, inexperienced boss

Some bosses are identified as inexperienced if there's a general consensus that they have been promoted too early and show signs of insecurity in their role. A reluctance to confront problems will also make them appear weak and ineffectual. These kinds of managers seem to be unhappy about being managers. Alternatively, they may have been in their jobs so long they have lost motivation and do not encourage staff to meet their objectives.

She won't lobby for the resources you need or stand up for you on critical issues. As a result, you are doing work below your own standards, but she doesn't seem to care—so long as it gets done within the budget and without upsetting anyone.

.

HOW IT AFFECTS YOU

1 There is no one to give you direction.

2 The boss has no idea of your workload.

3 You have no support on critical issues because the boss won't lobby for the resources you need.

4 A weak boss avoids conflict and that means you are being poorly supervised. Your motivation levels are likely to suffer.

5 The boss's eager-to-please manner encourages difficult behavior in others and maybe even incites petty rivalries.

6 The boss avoids taking risks because it may put her position in jeopardy.

Weak, inexperienced boss continued

HOW TO REACT

1 Avoid suggesting contentious or highly charged issues
as these are likely to worry a boss who needs to be liked
by everyone.

2 Let her know how you're feeling. She may pretend not to
notice there's trouble among colleagues, but a gentle
reminder, preferably in writing, makes it more difficult for her
to ignore.

3 Try to establish a mechanism for getting direction by insisting
on weekly or monthly meetings.

4 See it as an opportunity to become more of a self-starter and a decision maker. Become good at giving yourself feedback by setting milestones and evaluating regularly your effectiveness in meeting targets. You'll be able to put this new skill into practice the day you become a boss.

5 Whenever possible, try to resolve conflicts yourself. Cover yourself by sending an email to the boss and any other relevant work colleagues.

5

dealing with difficult

employees

Are you a difficult boss?

Bosses tend to be greatly outnumbered by their employees. Therefore they have a far greater chance of confronting difficult behavior. For a better understanding of the various types of problematic behavior you are likely to face, it's important to be aware of your own obligations and responsibilities as a paid leader. Try looking at yourself from the point of view of your staff. Could you in fact be a difficult boss? An honest answer to the following questions could provide you with a greater insight into your role and how you are perceived.

1 Do you understand the tasks and responsibilities of all your employees?

2 Do you have a reasonable idea of the progress each employee is making?

3 Do you hold periodic performance reviews?

4 Are you aware of your employees' ambitions?

5 Are you happy delegating work?

6 Do you rely on a few trusted employees to inform you how the rest of the staff is doing instead of looking at individual performance yourself?

Are you a difficult boss? continued

7 Do you encourage staff to talk to you about their problems?

8 Do you encourage staff to go on training courses?

9 How many employees have resigned in the last six months or so?

10 How often do you hold meetings?

11 Are you worried about not getting your own way?

12 Are you jealous of employees who suggest a better way of doing something? Are you feeling undermined by your own subordinates?

13 Do you exhibit traits that you frown on in your staff? If you think people are difficult because they are late for work or tell white lies, have they learned this behavior from you?

What makes a good boss?

Understanding the qualities employees are looking for in their supervisors can help you understand what is worrying or frustrating workers. Their responses to how you are not meeting their needs may give you clues to the sources of their difficult behavior. What is the job description generally expected of a manager?

TO ASSIGN AND CHECK WORK

Are you clear about what role you expect each worker to fulfill? Do you have a mechanism in place to determine if they are completing their task? Are you effectively communicating your requirements?

If you are not spelling out your objectives to your employees, it is very difficult for them to give you the standard of work and service you demand. This sets up a lose-lose situation, which satisfies no one.

TIPS FOR ASSIGNING AND CHECKING WORK

1 Learn to communicate your goals whether it is through meetings, regular emails, memoranda, or one-on-one chats. That way you'll avoid typical pleas of ignorance like: "I had no idea that was the deadline. Nobody told me. Was it up on the board?" "If you had told me you wanted it done that way, I would have followed your instructions."

2 Keep a detailed list of employees, their strengths and weaknesses, and how long they have been in the company. That way when a new assignment or project comes up, you can quickly decide who to pass the work on to based on recent evidence and availability. Employees are more likely to be impressed with your hands-on knowledge of their work.

3 Play to team members' strengths, while developing their competence in other areas. Don't rely on the same team members to fulfill tried and tested roles, but assign work to people who need to try something new. Establish a training culture, in which developing new competencies is expected and encouraged. Use the people you have, rather than buying in, if at all possible.

What makes a good boss? continued

TO ASSESS PERFORMANCE

Assessing employee performance is a key management job and one that will help you deal with difficult situations. First, if you make it clear what you expect from your employees, they are less likely to complain that they did not know what to do or how to do it. Second, assessing performance, especially in the context of an appraisal, creates a forum for airing grievances.

1 Do you have a system to monitor employees' progress?

2 Are appraisals done on a regular basis?

3 Do you tend to praise employees or only choose to communicate properly when something is wrong?

TIPS FOR ASSESSING PERFORMANCE

1 Have at least one annual performance appraisal, one every six months if possible as a year can be a long time to wait for feedback, especially if the employee is new.

2 When carrying out appraisals, don't linger on subjective subjects like initiative, judgment, or attitude. These are extremely difficult to quantify and can become highly personal.

3 Focus on planned objectives and seek evidence for how employees met their targets. This emphasis on hard facts makes it much easier for boss and employee to spell out exactly what has been achieved and where there is room for improvement.

What makes a good boss? continued

TO MOTIVATE EMPLOYEES

Encouraging personnel is one of a boss's key responsibilities. When a boss does little to motivate his workforce, it causes dissatisfaction in the workplace.

Have you thought of the different reasons why your employees are doing their job? Some may be doing it for the money and the bonus, others relish a challenge, some want the status of a job, others want a bigger office, some are chasing awards, others simply want job security.

Are your expectations realistic? Do you treat them as clever, rational people who can make their own decisions, or do you mistrust them in general and believe that unless you take control, they will produce no work? Very often, your expectations of employees mirror their actual performances and behavior. Demand high standards of them, and you are more likely to encourage hard work. Staff will meet and probably exceed your expectations in such as climate.

TIPS FOR MOTIVATING EMPLOYEES

1 Keep away from negative statements. If there is room for improvement, let them know first where they have achieved their targets and suggest ways in which they can improve on those. Some people, once branded as ineffective, lose so much self-confidence and goodwill that they justify future negative criticism of their work by the boss.

2 Credit them for good work done. Be specific with the compliments. The employee will be pleased that you have noticed and will continue trying.

3 When goals have been met, shift the goalposts to bolster ambition. This works best for the more productive workers. For the slower employees, it is important to be realistic about the rate of improvement.

What makes a good boss? continued

4 Let employees know how they have contributed to the company's general performance and provide some examples.

5 Encourage employees to seek the training they think will most benefit them and their jobs. Next, persuade your bosses that appropriate training courses will benefit the company. Make sure that it's not only the keen candidates who go to train. The more self-effacing employee would also benefit from external input.

6 Don't be afraid to ask employees for advice. It helps them feel included in the decision-making process, and they could come up with some interesting ideas that more senior managers have overlooked.

7 Provide financial incentives if certain targets are met. However, you might want to be discreet about bonuses as it might discourage those workers who fail to receive any bonus at all. A bonus that can be shared by an entire department, for instance, may be fairer than singling out an individual.

TO GAIN ACCEPTANCE OF CHANGE

Change, whether it is a change of office or a new style of management, is generally met with resistance by people, at least initially. It is up to the manager to ensure that the resistance is short-lived and doesn't become a source of difficult behavior.

THERE ARE GENERALLY THREE PHASES DURING A PERIOD OF CHANGE:

1

RESISTANCE
Employees, even those who disliked the old system, oppose the breaking of old habits. They may fear a change in the hierarchy within the department or extra demands on their working day.

2

RE-EDUCATION
Employees may not be aware that they are learning a new method of working because they are too busy resisting it. Effective communication and training will gradually bring the workforce around to implementing new ways.

3 ACCEPTANCE
Once the new system is operating satisfactorily, employees are doing their best to fit in with the new system.

TIPS FOR GAINING ACCEPTANCE OF CHANGE

1 Communicate the cons of the old system and the pros of the new one.

2 Inform employees of the direct benefits to them and the business of a new system.

3 Ask for feedback. This gives employees the feeling that they were part of the decision, even if they were not.

What makes a good boss? continued

4 Ask employees for constructive feedback during the transition process. It is harder for the die-hards to focus too much on resistance when they are being asked to participate in the change process.

5 Anticipate objections that will be raised.

6 Keep asking questions to get to the bottom of why certain people are resisting the change. It may be that in former positions in different companies change was badly handled. In other words, resistance has nothing to do with the changes you are currently proposing.

7 Try to identify the employees who are embracing the change and see if they can be recruited to promote the new system in a persuasive way.

8 Think of examples where competitors have made similar changes with successful results and make employees aware of them. There must be negative examples too of companies that resisted change and closed down as a result. Employees should be aware of them too.

9 Once the system has been in place for a few months, inform staff of tangible improvements.

What makes a good boss? continued

TO DELEGATE

Bosses can be notoriously poor at delegating work because either they don't trust others to do the work or they want to retain total control. There may even be cases where they don't know enough about their employees to decide who to delegate work to.

SOME COMMON EXCUSES ARE

1 "If I give this task to x, I'm going to have to take time to train them and also to check that it has been done correctly, so I may as well do it myself."

2 "I may not want to admit this but what if he does a better job than I do? I had better not take that risk."

3 "If he makes a mistake, I will be the one to blame."

ADVANTAGES OF DELEGATING WORK

1 You can train a trusted employee to take on a greater share of the department's responsibility, especially when you are not in the office.

2 You may have more chances of promotion because you have groomed a candidate to take over your role in the future.

3 You'll be leading a motivated staff that feels fulfilled, not reined in, by their role.

4 With a team of employees contributing the achievement of goals, you'll have many more opportunities to be successful.

5 You can simply get more done.

Difficult employee behavior

ABSENTEEISM

The number of workers absent from work due to sick leave has risen in recent years. The reasons are various: Some workers are so worried about keeping their jobs during a period of downsizing that they work even when they are not well and end up making themselves seriously ill.

They may also infect colleagues; a growing number of workers now take sick days to mitigate the stress of long hours and low levels of staff. The company ends up incurring costs in finding replacements, often at higher rates than the absent workers and overtime to try and make up for lost time. Part-time replacements, through no fault of their own, often need a period of training before they are up to speed with the rest of the team.

Sick leave of course is acceptable when an employee is genuinely unwell. But sick leave can also be abused, causing problems for you and your team.

WHAT TO DO

1 Remind staff exactly how many sick days they are allowed officially.

2 Ask any staff member who is sick for three days or longer to produce a doctor's certificate. Explain that he or she is not being singled out but that you are merely following company policy.

3 Work out if there is a pattern among workers who take sick leave. Are they suffering from stress? You might save valuable time and money in setting up a meeting that unearths the root of their absenteeism.

Difficult employee behavior continued

4 You could hint that a regular pattern of sick days is preventing you from being able to recommend a promotion. This is aimed at motivating employees to improve their record.

5 When you suspect that an employee is taking an excessive amount of sick days for invalid reasons, let them know in what ways their absence is causing problems in the department.

6 If this doesn't work, you could try calling them at home at the end of the working day and appear concerned about their illness. Gauge when they expect to be better.

7 In extreme cases, where absenteeism continues for an unprecedented long period of time, make careful notes on the case and issue them a warning.

Difficult employee behavior continued

LONG LUNCH/COFFEE BREAKS

Particularly in the service industries, lunch meetings are often the venue for brokering a deal, hatching a new project, or renewing invaluable contacts.

However, long breaks in the work schedule can be abused and cause resentment among colleagues who are not taking long lunch breaks themselves.

WHAT TO DO

1 Have a logbook where employees who are going on a lunch meeting write down whom they are meeting and where. Lead by example and do this yourself.

2 When the employee returns from their lunch meeting, express an interest and ask questions of what was discussed or achieved.

3 In jobs where there are no lunch meetings and workers take longer than allocated time, you can send a memo reminding the workers of company policy regarding time off for breaks. Don't single an employee out unless there is a regular pattern.

4 Encourage employees to get straight back to work after a meeting. Try to reduce the wind-up or wind-down before and after a meeting.

Difficult employee behavior continued

PERSONAL CALLS/EMAILS

When a large number of employees are in front of their computers all day, it becomes difficult to monitor the time they may spend on the Internet or the phone for personal reasons. It is also sometimes impossible to gauge how much these factors affect the flow of work. When dozens of emails are coming in to employees, chances are that some are going to be personal: You need to decide how to react to this.

WHAT TO DO

1 With personal calls, ask employees to limit these to practical arrangements and not to use them for long conversations.

2 If they haven't taken the hint, you could ask the receptionist to insist on callers, even familiar ones, to introduce themselves and ask for their reason for calling. In cases of real abuse, the receptionist could be asked to monitor the number of incoming personal calls.

3 You might (may) decide that use of email can be discretionary, but make sure you've laid down some ground rules. For instance, make it clear that emails at work are not confidential and that messages may be monitored regularly. Let workers know that the privilege of personal emails will be removed if it's used excessively.

4 Beware of the office jokers. Email can provide them with a new and immediate channel to spread dirty jokes that may be funny to their close friends but offensive to some colleagues. Prevent any potential problems by forbidding the transmission of inappropriate material, especially of sexual or violent nature.

Difficult employee behavior continued

CLOCK WATCHING

Employees are entitled to a healthy work/life balance and are becoming more vocal about demanding it. However, clock-watchers who seem to stop working the minute the big hand gets to 5 p.m. can cause conflict with those whose workload demands that they stay longer on occasion. The reverse scenario, where the same people are regularly in early or on time, while others are habitually late, can be equally divisive. Public transportation can be unreliable, but being late every day cannot be blamed wholly on transportation problems.

WHAT TO DO

1 It's wise to check why these people are so keen to leave the office early and whether it's affecting their productivity. They may be ultra-efficient and quick during the normal working day. Or they have families to pick up.

2 You should also ask yourself whether those who linger for hours after work are really time-wasters. Are they being inefficient during the day?

3 If you suspect an employee is underperforming because she is not putting in enough hours, suggest gently that to achieve her deadline, she may have to put in a few extra hours. You can volunteer drawing up a timetable for her if necessary. She is likely to take the hint.

Difficult employee behavior continued

MAKING CONSTANT MISTAKES

All employees are prone to errors. It's part of learning about a new job or project.

Making mistakes becomes a problem when it becomes consistent and the norm.

WHAT TO DO

1 Try to isolate the reasons for the causes of errors.

2 Once identified, don't criticize directly. Point out that to improve further on a task, it would be beneficial for the employee to take certain steps. Use a phrase like: "It would be useful if you could spend more time on x."

3 What part has your role as supervisor played? Have the tasks been adequately explained? Have you given the appropriate type of supervision? Could the employee be overworked?

A concern about an error-prone worker descends into a major problem when you've identified that the employee is simply out of his depth. Once again, you have to ask yourself the part you may have played in creating this scenario.

ASK YOURSELF

1 Do I need to organize some more training?

2 Did I overestimate his capabilities when I employed him?

3 Can I find a new role for the employee?

4 Can I find a replacement for the employee?

Difficult employee behavior continued

BEING TOO INDEPENDENT

Bosses like employees to show initiative, but those who show too much independence can prove to be a threat.

WHAT TO DO

1 Before acting, bosses should ask themselves if they want to encourage less personal initiative because they see it as a challenge to their leadership and ego or because the individual is genuinely upsetting the department and productivity.

2 In the latter case, you could try alerting your employee without discouraging future initiative: "We admire your efforts and we want to take up some of your ideas. However there are reasons why it may not work. Have you thought of...?" or "By all means, let's try your idea out. But we should take into consideration...."

Difficult employee behavior continued

BEING TOO SLOW

An employee may be holding up an entire department for taking longer than planned on her part of an assignment.

WHAT TO DO

1 It's fair for you to first check what exactly is causing the bottleneck. Was the employee given an unrealistic amount of work to do?

2 Was the employee trained for the job? Does she get on badly with the team so is deliberately delaying? Does the employee have difficulties making decisions and carrying them through?

3 The onus is on the boss to explain, before a major assignment, the exact nature of the job and the requirements. When there is a delay, the boss should also be able to suggest ways of speeding up the project.

4 The boss may also decide to relocate the slow worker elsewhere in the department.

Difficult employee behavior continued

POINTING THE FINGER

Employees can easily shift blame for a job that hasn't been completed, especially if the boss is hands-off and knows little of the details of a project or how its timeframe will work.

WHAT TO DO

1 It's up to the boss to discourage employees from passing the buck. Explain that any disciplinary action for work not completed will be fair.

2 Make sure that the levels of stress in the particular department are not unusually high and that's why people are more ready to blame a co-worker for any mistakes.

3 Work harder to create a culture in which blame is not the first recourse. When a project hits a problem, staff need to know that it will be managed, and that they will not be blamed.

4 Foster collaboration and teamwork: In a culture where staff feel they are all in it together, finger pointing is less likely.

5 Advocate for personal accountability and shared responsibility. Most people respond when they believe they have a personal stake in success.

Difficult employee behavior continued

DAYDREAMING

When employees have done the same job for a long time or lack motivation to improve, they are prone to daydreaming. This leads to errors and failure to reach targets.

WHAT TO DO

1 Encourage more initiative by asking what the employee would like to change about the way he is doing the job.

2 Sometimes you just have to let the employee go. Do this after you've explained how his daydreaming is affecting company targets and given him options to change.

3 Give him some extra work that he finds interesting and challenging.

4 When the boredom is chronic, ask him whether it is time to change departments. Be interested in how each member of your staff wants to promote him- or herself.

Difficult employee behavior continued

BEING DISHONEST

Fiddling expenses or taking company stationery home are two of the most common cases of employee dishonesty. Those who practice this form of theft tend to excuse it as a perk, an entitlement for working hard, or compensation for a low salary, or simply shrug it off as something that most employees practice.

WHAT TO DO

1 Monitor the frequency of the huge expenses or the disappearance of company materials. When you determine if it has become excessive, it may be time to issue a memo warning workers in general of the company policy toward dishonesty.

2 Approach a suspect only when you have firm, incontrovertible evidence.

3 State clearly what amounts are considered reasonable by the company to spend on taxis and lunches. Make sure you practice what you preach.

4 Keep one trusted person in charge of stationery. Ask employees to submit written requests for any extra material.

Difficult employee behavior continued

HIGH-MAINTENANCE EMPLOYEE

High-maintenance employees come in different guises, from talented perfectionists who require constant vigilance to ease their insecurities to prima donnas who simply crave attention. What they have in common is that they will demand a lot of a manager's time. Below are some ways of reducing the time supervisors have to devote to them.

WHAT TO DO

1 Learn to distinguish early on between the type of high-maintenance employee who is a valuable and long-term asset to the company and the one who, in spite of his contribution, wreaks too much havoc for you and other employees.

2 If you decide the employee is worth keeping, you might assign another senior supervisor to him to share the time-burden.

3 Establish boundaries. Set a regular time for feedback during the week. Make sure the employee knows this is a time when he will be listened to attentively. This will force both parties to prepare for meetings in an organized manner. During the meeting, listen attentively, and use feedback to let him know you have taken in his needs. Don't be afraid to let him know that he has to respect this time and not demand further meetings outside this allocated space.

4 Encourage the employee when he manages to cut back on the number of times he interrupts you or seeks advice or input by letting him know the benefits to the organization.

5 Nurture a team spirit. Let the high-maintenance person know he is operating in a team so that his work is not being judged on an individual basis but as a team effort. Hopefully, the difficult person will learn to approach others in his team and not rely solely on you as a manager.

Dealing with peer-to-peer problems

Difficulties between co-workers of equal standing present a particular set of challenges because there is no direct reporting relationship between them, and managers can't be seen to be dictating to them. Here are the most common cases of difficult peer behavior and some ways to tackle them.

AGGRESSIVE COMPETITORS

WHAT THEY DO

Competition against rival companies is healthy and motivating, but when overachievers encourage competition within a work team, even for the most trivial of tasks, it can turn petty at best and nasty at worst.

HOW TO REACT

It can be tempting to accept each challenge an aggressive co-worker puts your way, but you're only encouraging the over-achiever's behavior, making it more difficult to stop when you no longer want to take part. Be assertive from the start, showing you're not interested in office challenges. Suggest a game of sport after work. If the aggressive person continues to insist or is bullying another colleague into competitive games, use feedback, letting the person know exactly how her behavior is affecting the team's competitive advantage against rival companies.

NIT-PICKERS

WHAT THEY DO
Moaners exist in every office at all levels in an organization, often shifting their own dissatisfaction with themselves into sniping or negative criticism of others. They can resent colleagues who have a positive outlook on their work and life in general and drag down morale very quickly.

HOW TO REACT
Don't try to argue with them. That's showing them their remarks have touched you and will encourage them to try again. Try calm acknowledgment of their criticism, for instance by pretending to agree with some of their statement: "We may have got some of the figures wrong."

RESPONSIBILITY SHIRKERS

WHAT THEY DO
Some co-workers are expert at coasting along, allowing you to take the responsibility for work you both have to accomplish. Common ploys include being frequently late, spending a lot of time away from their desks, or taking a lot of time over one piece of work.

HOW TO REACT
Steer away from any personal criticism, focusing instead on a particular assignment where the outcome was affected by a series of difficulties. Make a written list of the problems so that you can be direct about them and suggest ways in which the problems can be solved.

Managing former colleagues

Few situations can be as problematic as having been promoted over a former co-worker, especially if that individual was also competing for the same job.

WHAT TO DO

1 If the co-worker is a close friend, be direct with him and raise the subject. That helps to clear the air. Maybe the close colleague is more concerned about what the promotion means to your relationship than the fact that you are now in a position of more responsibility.

2 Don't start acting differently. Be assertive and make clear what you intend to do with your new role and what you expect from others.

3 Take a resentful colleague aside and explain that you are counting on his ideas and follow-through to produce good results.

4 Conduct yourself at all times with professionalism. A former colleague's resentment, frustration, or envy is not your problem but his.

dealing with difficult employees

Managing internal battles

Employees who fail to co-operate are likely to slow you down.

WHAT TO DO

1 Nip the situation in the bud. Invite both parties to a meeting and tell them how their clashes are upsetting other colleagues and the outcome of a project.

2 Ask them to each identify their concerns. Listen carefully to both parties. Make notes that show them that you are concerned. The notes will be useful if the dispute continues at a later date.

3 Don't take sides. Summarize each position and suggest a few possible solutions.

4 Let them know that if the internal battles continue, you may have to take disciplinary action.

5 Keep the paperwork up to date. If the dispute escalates and you have to involve human resources, your records should be faultless. If it comes to law, you need to have good backup.

Managing difficult meetings

Conducting a successful meeting is quite a challenge. You have to make sure all participants make a valuable contribution while trying to make sure that the meeting runs smoothly and to time. In all likelihood, the same personality types that cause problems in everyday working life will rear their heads in a meeting where they can get more attention. The following are examples of difficult behavior in meetings and how to challenge them:

BEING ARGUMENTATIVE

WHAT THEY DO
They are ready to pounce on any idea or suggestion they disagree with. They hold up the meeting by stirring up debate.

WHAT YOU DO

1 Be patient and listen. If they don't think you are taking them into consideration, they'll be encouraged to continue the argument.

2 Acknowledge their point and then move on as quickly as possible. Try a phrase like: "Thanks for your contribution. Can we now turn to point x?" or "What is the relevance to our main concerns?"

3 If they still want to continue, ask other members if they think the point is worth pursuing. Unless everyone is moved by the subject, the lack of interest should bring an end to the argumentative interruption.

Managing difficult meetings continued

BEING SILENT

WHAT THEY DO

They look bored and are unwilling to contribute. Sometimes it's difficult to work out if they are shy or contemptuous of others.

WHAT YOU DO

1 Enforce that people speak their minds in rotation around the table. It doesn't look like you're singling the quiet ones out, but they'll be forced to make some contribution.

2 Direct questions at them from time to time. Don't make it obvious that you are picking on them.

JOKING AROUND

WHAT THEY DO

They use the meeting to exhibit their comic skills. They mock others' contributions, stop others from joining in, and cause delays.

WHAT YOU DO

1 Give a quick smile—just to acknowledge a joke. You don't want to appear priggish in front of the others. Then quickly resume business.

2 If jokes are offensive or inappropriate, simply state: "Those kinds of jokes can be saved for another occasion." You don't want to encourage any further interruptions.

Managing difficult meetings continued

PERFECTIONISM

WHAT THEY DO
They like to follow rules and can interrupt presentations by pointing out errors of fact or of procedure.

WHAT YOU DO

1 Thank them for their contributions and suggest that you want to focus on the general implications or directions of a point, rather than the specifics.

2 If you are holding the presentation, show the nit-picker a copy beforehand. Hopefully, any errors are picked up before the meeting.

WHISPERING

WHAT THEY DO

There are almost always people in meetings who are making barely audible remarks to a nearby colleague.

WHAT YOU DO

1 Stare at them to make sure you are aware that they are whispering.

2 Interrupt the proceedings and ask the whisperers to repeat what they are saying. Try a phrase like: "That sounds interesting. Would you like to share it with the rest of us?"

dealing with difficult employees

Dealing with a disappointing recruit

A final difficult employee problem is dealing with an individual whom a manager has personally appointed but who fails to live up to expectations. It's wise for managers to ask themselves what role they could have played in making a poor judgment rather than blame the new appointment.

QUESTIONS TO ASK

1 Did you do enough detailed research into the person's background?

2 Did you check the references?

3 Has an aspect of the job or the industry changed since the recruitment?

4 Did the person mislead you during the interview?

5 Do you have to improve your recruitment methods?

6 Can you improve matters with some training?

Tips for successful meetings

A further way of countering difficult behavior during meetings is excellent preparation.

1 Let all participants know what the meeting is about before the meeting. Underline the importance of the meeting to push a new project forward or to find a solution to a problem. Remind them at the start of the meeting what you are discussing and set a timeframe.

2 Ask one participant to take notes. That way there can be no quibble at a later date as to what was discussed. If you anticipate one of the participants is likely to be a troublemaker, get her to take the notes. It will keep her out of mischief and make her feel important.

3 Let participants know you hope to come to an agreement on most points. Let them know you are open to constructive discussion. That way attendants feel they have a role to play in the process and that the outcome hasn't been predetermined. It may encourage them to contribute more.

4 Don't let the focus of the meeting steer away from your original plan. If someone raises an important but unrelated point, make sure you acknowledge the contribution and show that you appreciate the input. Try to move swiftly on but first make sure that you arrange to debate the subject at another time.

5 Wrap up the meeting with a conclusion that covers all points discussed.

6 Send a written summary of the meeting to the participants. They will take any agreements more seriously, and it will help to clarify any misunderstandings. Try to include some forward-looking statements in the summary so that everyone is left with a sense of purpose.

dealing with difficult
customers

Put yourself in the customer's shoes

The best way to understand problematic customers is to remember that you too are likely to be a regular customer of a variety of products and services. Unless you're extremely lucky, you must know what it's like to get upset with indifferent service or a disappointing product. Remember how you like to be treated as a customer and that will help you confront clients who are angry and dissatisfied. Some characteristics that most people value about good customer service follow.

1 The customer is first. Customers keep business afloat. Their needs are a priority. Shopping attendants or, increasingly likely these days, telephone customer service officers are not doing clients a favor by helping them.

2 Customers expect fast, efficient service.

3 Customers expect company representatives to have a thorough understanding of the services and products they are offering.

4 Customers like to think their queries or demands are special to staff.

5 Customers appreciate sales reps who anticipate their needs and are able to offer useful alternatives or suggestions.

Common customer complaints

1 They are left waiting at a restaurant while new arrivals are seated.

2 When they're on the phone, they're kept on hold for a long time.

3 If they are not kept on hold, then they are passed from department to department in vain. Having to repeat their complaint afresh each time only aggravates the original grievance.

4 They are ignored at a department store. The staff are too busy chatting.

5 They are hounded in a shop after they've politely told attendants they will ask for help it if they need it.

6 A hotel receptionist can't find the hotel reservation they made weeks ago.

7 The product they ordered over the Internet is the wrong color and size.

8 Their valuable purchase doesn't work.

Dealing with customer feelings

Being adept at handling angry customers has many benefits. Research shows that the majority of customers who feel dissatisfied with the way they've been treated, don't complain. They take their business elsewhere. Angry customers care enough to complain and are highly likely to continue doing business with your company if handled effectively. That's why they are customers worth saving.

POINTS TO REMEMBER

1 The most typical reaction of a dissatisfied customer is frustration and then anger. Unless you handle the customer with care, the anger can easily escalate into rage. Ways to take the heat out of a potentially problematic situation start on page 220.

2 Not only are there benefits to your company, but you personally gain as well. Become adept at handling angry customers, and you'll feel much more confident in your own abilities. Anyone can work with easy people, but it takes a real professional to be successful with difficult customers. Also, difficult customers who are satisfactorily placated by excellent customer service usually feel a new sense of loyalty toward the company and its products or services.

3 Don't take it personally. The customer is blue with rage about another part of the company that doesn't involve you. On the other hand, it may be the result of a mistake you made. In both cases, remember that the customer is annoyed with the faulty product or service. It's not a personal attack on you. Try also not to hold it against them if they don't smile. They are not your friends. Try to understand their viewpoint and do your best to help. Remain detached, and you can proceed with attending to the customer's issues, not your own feelings.

Dealing with customer feelings continued

LISTEN

It seems obvious but often, customers' main complaint beyond their specific problem, is that "nobody listens to them." The longer they feel they are not being acknowledged, the more time they'll spend detailing their complaint. Many irate customers may be feeling rejection and need some attention. Give it to them early on, and you may have to spend less time in the long run trying to placate them. How do you show the customer that you are really listening to the complaint?

1 Don't interrupt unless you are checking to verify a certain point or word you don't understand.

2 Repeat what the person is saying in your own words to make sure you've got it right. For example say:s "Just to make sure I've understood. You're saying that..." or "Excuse me, could you clarify that last point?"

3 If you are in a noisy environment, you might ask them to step aside to continue in a more private room.

4 Use body language to show you are hanging on to the customer's every word. For instance, lean your body slightly forward, nod your head at regular intervals, and establish and maintain eye contact.

5 Don't answer any phone calls if at all possible.

6 Taking notes helps customers feel you are taking them seriously. It helps you to make sense of their complaint. It also provides a useful reference if the problem can't be resolved immediately and you need to relay the information to a superior.

Dealing with customer feelings continued

ACKNOWLEDGE

Listening is the first part. Next you have to show you are acknowledging what the customer is saying.

1 Show sympathy. Try to see the situation from their perspective. It is your job to try and understand the source of their frustration. When you do that, you are letting them know they are important to the company. It only takes a few select words like "I'm very sorry to hear that" or "I can understand how difficult this must have been for you" to show you are making the effort to see the situation from their point of view.

2 Don't forget that showing sympathy does not mean you are agreeing with them. Nor are you accepting that the customer is right. The main objective is to take the heat out of the moment by showing some understanding.

STAY NEUTRAL

At this early stage, it is not appropriate to come to any conclusions either in favor of or against the customer.

If you start defending the company or a colleague or yourself by explaining your problems, customers won't be interested. They will also think you are trying to steer away from their main concern. You don't want to agree with customers' complaints either. You don't want to give customers the false impression that you are going to resolve the issue immediately when you can't guarantee it.

Wait until you are sure of all the facts before answering the concern.

CLARIFY

Once the customers have finished their complaint, even if you are clear on the major points, it's useful to summarize what you've heard back to them.

To make sure you haven't misunderstood what you have been told, try using phrases such as:

"What you are telling me is that...Is that correct?"

"There are three main points then. Have I missed anything?"

Dealing with customer feelings continued

FIND A SOLUTION

Now that you've identified the problem, you are in a position to try to find a solution, even if it is only temporary.

1 Make customers feel they are involved in the solution-finding process. Try open questions like: "What would you like me to do to take this forward?" "How exactly can we help you?"

You don't necessarily have to agree with the customers' opinions about how to proceed. The important thing is that you make the customers participants and find what solution they would like implemented. Then you can work out how their wishes square with the reality of company policy.

2 You can apologize. This doesn't have to be interpreted as an acknowledgment of wrongdoing. It can merely be a further way of showing empathy. The phrase "I am sorry this has happened to you" is neutral. You are neither blaming the customer nor the company.

Show that you are trying to come to a solution that best suits the client. Your strategy should be to arrive at a solution that will be positive for both your company and the customers.

Dealing with customer feelings continued

3 When you are confident about how far you can go to satisfy your customers, provide them with a couple of alternatives that come closest to their desired objective.

4 If you are in any doubt about how to proceed or you need confirmation from another colleague or a supervisor, let the customers know you have understood their problem and that you will do your best to see that the relevant people are informed.

5 In the event of not being able to offer any kind of immediate solution, don't just tell the customer you are unable to meet their needs. Explain that you are trying to do your best for them and take down their details so that you can keep them informed. Try a phrase like: "This sounds like a very important concern, so I am going to need some more time to get to the bottom of this."

Dealing with customer feelings continued

FOLLOW THROUGH

This is the most important stage of dealing with complaints because it is what the customers will most remember. You have to deliver what you promised, even if it is to give them unsatisfactory news or to explain that the matter requires more time. When you can't offer the sort of resolution they were seeking, try to provide some sort of compensation if possible. For example: "We can't provide you with this service, but we would be happy to offer a discount on a similar product."

CHECK BACK

The checkback is your opportunity to make sure that the customers are satisfied and feel good about the resolution. Always check back: It is the only way you are going to get a resolution. Not only does it make the customers feel good, but it reflects well on both you and the organization. Customer care is what differentiates one company from another. On the opposite page are examples of checkbacks to use.

1 "Does that sound reasonable?"

2 "Do you think that makes sense?"

3 "Have you been satisfied with the inquiry?"

It's also a chance to let the customers know that the company is making every effort not to repeat a mistake.

In addition, once customers have verified that they are happy, it is difficult for them to come back with a further problem.

Dealing with customer feelings continued

DEALING WITH SPECIFIC DIFFICULT BEHAVIOR

PROBLEM: A CUSTOMER WHO SCREAMS IN PUBLIC

1

WHAT TO DO:
Don't scream back. Don't make threats like "Unless you stop shouting, I won't be able to attend to you." This will only make the situation worse. Invite the screamer to a more private setting. If she doesn't take the hint, point to the general direction of another room. Remain calm. Remember, the aggression is not personal.

PROBLEM: A CUSTOMER IS RUDE

2

WHAT TO DO:
Don't retaliate by being rude back and ignoring them. Don't reward the behavior by taking special notice either. A short but polite "What can I do to help you?" should force the customer to reconsider her approach. If the rudeness continues, ask her if she would like to talk to a manager. It's more difficult to be rude to more than one person. She may have to reconsider her behavior.

PROBLEM: A CUSTOMER USES SWEAR WORDS

3 WHAT TO DO:
A growing number of companies, even in the public service, are putting up notices stating that their employees should not accept unreasonable behavior. Swearing can be threatening. You can point out that you'll be glad to help if the customer desists from swearing, which is not accepted by company policy.

PROBLEM: A CUSTOMER WON'T TAKE NO FOR AN ANSWER

4 WHAT TO DO:
Remain calm. Have handy a phrase explaining politely why you can't oblige with the customer's demand. Repeat it several times if necessary. Use a phrase such as: "I can understand what you are saying, but these are the regulations." Try to provide alternatives, but not if the customer is being unreasonable.

dealing with difficult customers

Techniques on the telephone

A growing number of interactions with customers are on the phone.

TIPS FOR SATISFYING CUSTOMERS

1 Pick up the phone right away.

2 Identify yourself or the name of the company.

3 Let the caller know you are there to help them.

4 Always have a pen and paper to write down names and requests.

5 Paraphrase the message back to the caller to make sure that you have understood the message.

6 If you have a prerecorded message saying you are busy or out, try to get back to callers the same day.

7 When transferring calls, make sure that you let the receiver know the nature of the call.

8 Don't keep the caller on hold for longer than a minute and let them know that you are aware that they are being kept waiting, especially when the minute is up.

9 When the client is shouting, it may be tempting to hang up. Interrupt calmly and backtrack. Try something like "You seem to be unhappy about x. How can I help you?"

Techniques on the telephone continued

10 If you are getting too intense with a difficult customer, get into a relaxed position. Try putting your feet up or leaning back.

11 Do you want to sound more commanding or assertive? Try talking from a position of strength. Stand up, spread your legs slightly to shoulder width. Remain upright.

12 When confronting an irate customer, be sure to take frequent, deep breaths.

13 To take the heat off the moment, try doodling or drawing a cartoon of the offending person at the end of the line.

14 To aid concentration, close your eyes.

15 Try not to send emails on the spur of the moment. Read them through, save them, and come back to them half an hour later unless they are straightforward or urgent; in that case, answer them right away.

16 Get a colleague to read an email that you think might be construed as controversial.

A R.C.L. 2006